LONDON
PERCEIVED

LONDON PERCEIVED

A PORTRAIT OF THE CITY

V. S. PRITCHETT

DAUNT BOOKS

First published in hardback by Daunt Books in 2016
This edition reissued in 2022 by
Daunt Books
83 Marylebone High Street
London W1U 4QW

1

A CIP catalogue record for this title is available
from the British Library.

ISBN 978-1-914198-42-7

Typeset by Antony Gray
Printed and bound by TJ Books Limited
Cover design by Nathan Burton
Also available as an eBook

www.dauntbookspublishing.co.uk

INTRODUCTION

LIKE SO MANY LONDONERS I was not born in London, but I have lived in this city for more than eighty years. And although my father came from Yorkshire, my mother was indigenous. I was a child of the once-famous fogs, of train smoke and horse traffic, and I was sent to a dozen schools in my early boyhood, north and south of the Thames, as the family migrated from district to district. As a youth I was put to work in a Bermondsey hide and skin warehouse and got to know the markets, the wharves and docks, and was sent as a messenger, sometimes atop glorious horse-drawn vans, on fantastic and gloating journeys 'across the water', all over the City. I have played football in the parks, known the first air raids of the 1914 war and have been an addicted traveller of the London streets. In this pervasive sense London has been my university.

The present discursive evocation, written in 1962, springs out of a life-long passion. If by that time London was no longer the most powerful capital in the world, its historical and living enchantment remained, as it does still. It is one of the world's great markets; it is the birth place of the English language. If the power of the Victorian age – which held its spell and sway over London and Londoners in my own youth – has gone, and if London and Londoners have changed their scene and habits today, the place retains its liveable and incurable fundamental character.

In 1962 we were at a point of change, at least on the surface. I could not have known, for instance, that this was the moment when London would lose its low, almost Venetian skyline, that prison-like tower blocks would shoot up high and break so much of the spirit of locality on which the city's genius for intimacy – and the safety of it – depended. The little houses and their gardens, so calming and civilising to islanders given to outbursts of violence, were going. The Second World War and the destruction it had caused to the city streets had given shameless opportunities to a new wave of property developers; our architects, whether romantic or classical, were beginning to turn London into a neighbourless Megapolitan city. And perhaps the influence of that war led them to commission designers of block houses and strong-points, so that a theatre or an art gallery became more a prison or fortification preparing for street warfare or a shelter from missiles.

As I re-read this essay I notice that I was – as I am now – most interested in the character of Londoners as it has changed, or did not change, from century to century. If we were formal and buttoned up when I was young, the new crowd is popular, extravagant, informal and fantastic in its style, spontaneous to the point of being more like the explosive Elizabethans than other generations, even the Edwardian dandies. In a sense, the Londoner remains an actor playing a part – donning his mask, just as the apparently respectable Victorian of Dickens' time did and, indeed, as he has done down the centuries. I still think that the London mind has more back than front to it. Also like the Victorians, we are aware of living in a continuing social revolution. If we no longer have the mob, we have the chanting 'demo'. There is the great change of immigration from the Third World; there is the liveliness of colour. We are a bazaar. There is a new London dialect created by television. This language is no longer a reader's language.

But there is a more surprising change: for more than a century the foreigner used to come to London almost solely for trading reasons; to him, the notion of coming for ease and pleasure was laughable. London was simply standoffish. Now foreigners come in their millions to enjoy themselves; for the night life, the fashions, even for the cuisine; for the kindness of the pavements and the intimacies of the pubs and the abandon of the parks – in short, the continuing Londonishness of the place and its people. The very name of the city, as I said in this book, still has 'tonnage' in it.

V. S. Pritchett, London 1985

LONDON PERCEIVED

1

'How Do You Like London? . . . London, Londres, London?' Mr Podsnap asked the Frenchman, putting – we notice – capital letters into his accent. 'And Do You Find, Sir,' he went on, 'Many Evidences that Strike You . . . ?'

Nothing else but evidence strikes us. The place is all evidence, like the sight of a heavy sea from a rowing boat in the middle of the Atlantic where you are surrounded by everything and see nothing. But evidence of what? There is no possible answer. Except for the ant heap in Tokyo, London is the largest capital city in the world, and – one used to be told, though I do not know, or much care, how they measured these things – the largest seaport, and is, as Trollope said, unintelligible. One lives in it, afloat but half submerged in a heavy flood of brick, stone, asphalt, slate, steel, glass, concrete and tarmac, seeing nothing flexible beyond a few score white spires that splash up like spits of foam above the next glum wave of dirty buildings.

We can at any rate *place* this monstrous splodge and what Henry James called its 'horrible numerosity of society'. It lies substantially in a marsh between low chalk hills – the source of artesian water supply – ten minutes' flight from the clean air of the North Sea and some thirty miles up the Thames. As you fly into London you notice that the northern sunlight dims over the more than 700 square miles of the total conurbation; in the 117 square miles of the centre, it is common for the sun to vanish altogether. The daily average of sunlight for the year is three hours and twenty minutes. You come down under a grey ceiling into a variable light which encloses the mind at once. (Strangely, the only other city in the world with such a ceiling is the rainless city of Lima, in Peru, which lies under a grey Londonish cloud for half of every day.) This is the first intimation of the double London feeling that you are being driven in on yourself yet are secure and about to be nurtured; and its complement – that you will go mad if you do not get out. This will take some doing, for you are landing in a city twenty-five to thirty miles across in any direction, which has hundreds of miles of railway track, a subsoil riddled with underground railways, wires, pipes, sewers and tunnels, where the police jurisdiction runs as far as Brighton, fifty miles away, and which smokes gratuitously and pensively in your face.

One's first impression is of a heavy city, a place of aching heads. The very name London has tonnage in it. The two syllables are two thumps of the steam hammer, the slow clump-clump of a policeman's feet, the cannoning of shunting engines or the sound of coal thundering down the holes in the pavements of Victorian terraces. Lie down on the grass in the middle of a London park, far away from any street and from the numerosity, and the earth rumbles and trembles day and night. The note is low and ruminative and, in this, resembles the quiet but meaning voices of the people who hate drama more than anything else on earth and for reasons that do not totally bear inspection. As Londoners, we are – you see – drama itself and have no reason to whip ourselves up into states with sirens and altercations. We like the police to be quiet, the ambulances discreet, and the fire engines jolly.

This weight of the city and its name have other associations, mainly with the sense of authority, quiet self-consequence – known among us as modesty – unbounded worry, ineluctable usage and natural muddle. These are aspects of a general London frame of mind. If Paris suggests intelligence, if Rome suggests the world, if New York suggests activity, the word for London is experience. This points to the awful fact that London has been the most powerful and richest capital in the world for several centuries. It has been, until a mere thirty-five years ago, the capital of the largest world empire since the Roman and, even now, is the focal point of a vague Commonwealth. It is the capital source of a language now dominant in the world. Great Britain invented this language; London printed it and made it presentable. At the back of their minds – and the London mind has more back than front to it – Londoners are very aware of these things and are weighed down by them rather than elated. The familiar tone of the London voice is quick, flat-vowelled and concerned. The speaker is staving off the thought that hope is circumscribed and that every gift horse is to be looked at long in the mouth. He is – he complains – through no fault of his own, a citizen of the world. Half his mind, like that true Londoner, Antonio in *The Merchant of Venice*, is with his galleons overseas. And I do not speak only of the top people in Lloyd's, the Bank of England, Downing Street, Lambeth Palace or Buckingham Palace, or what we call the Establishment; I speak of the bus drivers, the office-workers, even the office cleaners. It is the man who is painting your house who tells you he 'sees' the French government has fallen, that the Congo is unsettled, or that there is a dock strike in New York or 'trouble' in the Middle East. Foreigners are the Londoner's nightmare; it is a nightmare he is paid to have every night when he goes to bed. Sometimes rather well paid. There can be few of London's nine millions who have not one close relative abroad and one at sea and who are not directly aware, like modest seismographs, of what is going on behind the scenes in places where the weather is better. They will mention the matter in pubs, lifts, at shop counters, in bus queues. The man who delivers my beer shuddered this week at the thought of what is going on in Iran: he once made a structural alteration in the Shah's Rolls-Royce, outside Teheran. The publican at the end of the street worked on a survey in Turkey: he worries about the Turks, economically, geographically. A local waiter can run you off a résumé of the financial prospect and political tangle in Singapore.

This is simply to say that London is before anything else the world's market, and that markets are as sensitive as opera singers. And this no doubt explains why London is the least splendid, the least ostentatious of the great capitals. Property is what it cares for. It has no definable style, though, as Henry James said, it has a succession of attempts at style. One might expect the centre, at any rate, to look imperial, to display itself in planned avenues sweeping rhetorically to splendid, monumental climax. We have hardly succeeded there; dictators can be splendid, democracies can swagger – parliaments cannot bear the expense. But for royalty and the aristocracy, up to the early nineteenth century, the whole of public London would be a leaseholder's warren. The merchants have always beaten down the planners; the mercantile mind cannot tolerate either vista or perspective. It is indispensable for traders to dwell, as Walter Bagehot said, in a twilight where no shapes, sizes and distances are defined. We have no rhetorical architecture at all, and it is notorious that when Sir Christopher Wren planned a new London after the Great Fire of 1666, he was defeated. The Houses of Parliament and Buckingham Palace are among the few great edifices to stand in sufficient space, compose a view, and dominate a distance. St Paul's, on its hill, is still shut in by the money-makers. Our only boulevards are the Mall and the Embankment of the river from Blackfriars to Chelsea; and though we have our monuments, palaces, mansions, formidable institutes, our rich art galleries and even a triumphal arch or two, these have been swallowed by the city. They are domesticated; they are never ornately imposed. We have been capable of building pretty squares but we are constitutionally incapable of the *grande place*.

I am aware of a hypocritical, false modesty in the word 'constitutionally'; the plain fact is the mercantile class that has owned London is now making gross fortunes by speculating in the rebuilding of it and is too greedy to be splendid. Londoners affect to despise money and put on gentlemanly airs about it, pretending to be old-fashioned, shabby, dilatory and above the whole thing when it comes to price; and here the famous English hypocrisy, the blue-eyed, rosy-cheeked Pecksniffery, is at its hottest. We may despise millions, we produce few misers and few reckless bidders for fortune or dispensers of it; but we are up all

8

night toiling away at acquiring and defending property. The Englishman's home is his castle – but what he is really interested in is the freehold. Dear, old-fashioned, leisurely, traditional, eccentric London is a legend we have successfully sold to foreigners – even to ourselves. London fails to look splendid because it is a hard place, as hard as nails.

No style – I turn to Henry James's *Notebooks*, the entry made in 1881 when he recorded his decision to give up Boston, his disillusion with Paris, and the judgement that London was the best place for him. He sat before his coal fire with the draught blowing down his back at Morley's Hotel – since pulled down – near Trafalgar Square, after a tortuous and rather horrible journey in a cab from the black Greek arch at Euston. (They have just pulled it down.) He has described his emotions in *English Hours*, and the chapters on London in that book evoke a city that, despite a fault here and there and the passage of time, is permanent. The *Notebooks*, being a diary, put the matter in brief:

It is difficult to speak adequately or justly of London. It is not a pleasant place; it is not agreeable, or cheerful, or easy, or exempt from reproach. It is only magnificent. You can draw up a tremendous list of reasons why it should be insupportable. The fogs, the smoke, the dirt, the darkness, the wet, the distances, the ugliness, the brutal size of the place, the horrible numerosity of society,

9

the manner in which this senseless bigness is fatal to
amenity, to convenience, to conversation, to good
manners – all this and much more you may expatiate
upon. You may call it dreary, heavy, stupid, dull,
inhuman, vulgar at heart and tiresome in form . . .
But . . . for one who takes it as I take it, London is on
the whole the most possible form of life.

The extraordinary thing is that, despite the blunder of the
splodge as a whole, life *is* wonderfully liveable in this city: so
much has been left to nature and human nature and
their privacies. After the first chills of loneliness, after their
unbelief before the climate, after their astonished failure to
find a congenial night life, foreigners usually astonish us by
coming to the same conclusion. They may not like us, but
they like the place. Since 1940 they have liked it enormously.
London has its immigrants who come for the money: the
West Indians, the Africans, the Indians, the Pakistani, the
Italians, the Cypriots, the Irish pour in. But more flattering
than these is the large and growing population of expatriates:
people getting out of the new, expanding, aggressive
countries with a future, a programme, and a zeal for
the human race. Americans, South Africans, Australians,
Canadians slip out of their societies and are added to the
Jews of the thirties, the Hungarians, Poles, Czechs, and so
on who wish to be left to live outside the reach of ideologues

and witch-hunters, and as they please. London loves the morbidities of freedom. It has been the traditional refuge from despotism and persecution from the seventeenth century onwards. Although Londoners are, more than any other city people, wary of foreigners, although London landladies are Britannias armed with helmet, shield, trident, and have faces with the word 'No' stamped like a coat of arms on them, the place is sentimental and tolerant. The attitude to foreigners is like the attitude to dogs: dogs are neither human nor British, but so long as you keep them under control, give them their exercise, feed them, pat them, you will find their wild emotions are amusing, and their characters interesting. They even have their own sometimes enviable life; they assume your habits and – such are the pleasures of British loneliness – they become a man's best friend. The Bayswater landlady gazes at her spaniel and says with proud complacency, 'He's trying to say something.' So is the foreigner. After a year or two of resentment, the foreigner recognises that London is a place where we are all mongrels together, mainly on leash, but let out for short, mad daily scampers in the park.

But perhaps the quality that does most to make London liveable is its respectability. This is often mocked, and there have been periods when respectability has been pushed to extremes; but after a lifetime of travel in Europe, Asia and America, I am convinced that to be respectable is one of the pinnacles of universal human desire, felt as strongly in the heart of the Persian nomad as it is in New York, Chicago, Valparaiso or Tooting Bec. And that London has very often known the art of concocting this subtle elixir.

I have made much of the weight of London and the muddled public aspect. It is time to correct the impression. Historically, London has grown not by planning, but by swallowing up the countryside village by village. It spread outside its medieval walls into the fields of Holborn, into the 'liberties' of the East End, the ruralities of Southwark, the village of Charing – called that because there the Thames made a 'char' or bend – and eventually met the religious settlement of Westminster expanding eastward to meet it. The muddle is simply a muddle of villages that eventually surround the parks of the kings. Go up to some green bump like Primrose Hill, close to the zoo, a mile and a half from Piccadilly, and look down. Throughout the summer London looks chiefly green, a forest broken here and there by a spire, a tower, a block of flats. One is in the country. It is difficult, anywhere, to be more than fifty yards from a tree. In the parks that stretch for many square miles from West-minster to Notting Hill and from Marylebone to Primrose Hill, and south of the river in Battersea – to speak only of the centre and to leave out the greenery of Hampstead or Blackheath and the deer park at Richmond – one might be a hundred miles from London. In our damp and lethargic air the grass grows lusciously, the trees grow tall and spreading. The terrace where I live, only a quarter of an hour's walk from Oxford Circus, is enclosed by a long lawn and I cannot see across the street to the main line from Euston because of the flaking plane trees, the seeding poplars, the weeping elms, the chestnuts. At the back, the scene is a jungle. We are hidden from one another by dozens of spreading planes and sycamores, fig trees – an old London party – plum trees and beech. The sight is tropical and dense. We feel the breath of leaves. I can walk on grass most of the way to Oxford Street, always in shade. Sheep graze in Regent's Park, the duck are on the lake, crows flop across, the hawk goes off to hover over rats on the river and at night the owls hoot in the gardens. In the evening under the nail-varnish pink of the artificial London sky, the trees blacken into a forest wall; one is walking in the cool of a long quiet twilight and, at some turns of the walk, the rumble of the place is cut off and one could be in the outer isles. Such a city is too countrified to be megalopolis. From the time of William the Conqueror, the Londoner has always been getting out, dragging London with him, of course, ruining the fields with the brick so easily made out of the London clay. Our poisoned soil is good for flowers and herbage. Hydrangeas and dahlias thrive in their seasons. In the spring the parks and squares are alight with crocuses. Dock-workers grow roses in the docks. They grow them in the middle of railway sidings, a yard from the fume of the diesel engine. Left to himself for half an hour, when the ship has tied up or the goods train is held by a signal, the docker or railway man will start gardening, as others play a short game of cards.

His instinct is to plant; his next instinctive move is to put a fence round what he has planted, even if it is only made of a few stones and only three inches high. He has created what he dreams of all the time: his country estate; and he will even take a walk in a place two yards long and probably feel 'the air is different'. For your benefit and with the ornate hypocrisy of the Cockney, he will put on a false Cockney pathos and even half a dishonest tear in one eye and say something about 'liking a bit of green', but in fact an old-style country squire himself could not be more determined and hard-headed about his acres. After the war, his memories of the bombing were deeply appeased by the sight of the miles of purple willow herb blooming over the ruins around London Wall. Nature was getting its own back on the city that had imprisoned him and, as an imaginary countryman, putative farmer and exhibitor at the Chelsea Flower Show, the man was glad. Not given to abstract thought, notoriously lacking in the impulses and the exacting sense of style that make the artist – disparaging art because it is not for him – he is a rudimentary Wordsworthian. Down in Billingsgate is the ancient church of St Magnus the Martyr, jammed between the Fish Market and the tall offices of New Fresh Wharf. In the yard, growing out of the stone, is one of those high heroic London trees, raising its sooty branches against the windows of the offices. Typewriters clatter among its branches instead of birds, and if a breeze gets down into that fishy hole, the sound of the leaves turning will be like the sound of the pages of ledgers being turned. I am sure that the tree is more admired than the beautiful carving of the church, and on Wordsworthian grounds. There are dozens of secret gardens in the City, wedged between the office blocks that have been there since the Fire. Nature is all, in its green summer gloss, but also in winter, when the millions of London trees are spectral and we walk down the avenues of the parks where the trees are like black processions of widows, going on and on until they vanish in the mist of all London vistas and the long sad sunsets.

The Londoner believes in nature and greenery, loves to walk under trees or lie in the parks with his arms round his girl to the scandal of puritanic foreigners, who see miles of park treated as a public bedroom and think the cult of nature carried too far; besides, they have been brought up on the peculiar foreign superstition that the English do not like love, the evidence being that they do not talk about it. In fact, northern passions are too strong for speech and too direct for literature. Mrs Patrick Campbell is reported to have said that you can do what you like in London as long as you don't do it in the street and don't frighten the horses; but you can do it in the parks, which each Londoner regards as his private estate. He is convinced that although he is cuddling only a yard from the path among ten thousand others, he is quite alone. The fence, the wall – that is a necessity for him, and if it doesn't exist in fact, he sees to it that it exists, as the saying is, psychologically.

London is millions of small chimneys, millions of Victorian door-pillars displaying the essence of private consequence. It is millions of windows and walls – what goes on inside them is not your business or mine. The feeling for seclusion goes very deep in the London character and is responsible for the intimacy of London life and for a system of abrupt protective manners that makes life very liveable. Of course, the compulsion may lead to extremes. It may turn out that the addict of privacy is called Christie, lives in that grim cul-de-sac called Rillington Place, and is quietly burying woman after woman in the rockery or the walls, year after year. What is amenity one moment may be murder. A lot 'goes on' in all large cities; in London it goes on behind the wall of a disarming face that has been given the *maquillage* of a self-respect which, somewhat often, is ingrained complacency and humbug. It would be easy to go on and present the Londoner as something of a snob, a smug fellow inclined to the sentimental and the vulgarly genteel and, if his reserve goes, given to licentiousness and brutality;

fulfilling that definition of a gentleman which says that a gentleman is one who is never rude except intentionally – and what an extravagant sight when that intention breaks through.

It is better to stick to the evidence offered by the streets, the squares, the buildings and by history. London excels in the things that segregate and preserve an air of privilege. The sense is historic and innate. Londoners are people with background. Every Londoner, from the dock-worker to the Duke of Edinburgh, belongs to some body of the like-minded. The thought was put in an old Cockney song:

> Last night a copper came dahn ahr Court;
> Nah the Pleece Force is one copper short.
> 'Old yer row – what did you s'y?
> We kills all the coppers that come dahn ahr w'y.

And in that notice seen in so many London institutions: Members Only. The Londoner is a member. He is in a state of tension between the convenience of being a member and an anarchic, libertarian instinct which violently mocks his own conformity. One might call him by nature a recalcitrant member. Again and again, London institutions are founded by groups of recalcitrants.

Historically, this appears in the early years of London, when it was two cities: the walled City founded by the Romans between the Tower of London and London Bridge, where the merchants and city rulers lived, and the Frenchified monastic settlement of Westminster, on its marsh, where the kings and bishops ruled. Each party stuck to the rights of the group of which he was a member. The Monarch had to ask permission of the Lord Mayor to enter the City. He still has to do so. At Temple Bar, in Fleet Street – the arch that marked the entrance was removed in late Victorian times – the Monarch still pauses to receive from the Mayor the symbolic key to the sacred square mile we call the City. Perhaps the feeling for membership grows from monasticism, for the friars – the Black Friars, Grey Friars, Austin Friars, Templars – built their houses outside the Roman wall. The lawyers followed them with their Inns. So that now the lovely Inns of Court – the Temple, Lincoln's Inn and Gray's Inn – extend in quadrangle, close and lawn, like the colleges of Oxford and Cambridge, from the river at Blackfriars northward to Holborn, west to the Strand. They bring a breath of quiet and dignity to a region where the business and traffic of London is heaviest. After the Inns came the mansions of the nobility along Fleet Street and the Strand, jealous centres of independent power in themselves; Essex Street, Norfolk Street, the Savoy Hotel, Buckingham Street, the fine water-gate to the Duke of Buckingham's palace, remind us of these. One is driving past the dramatic site of Shakespeare's histories. After the monasteries, the Inns, the palaces, come the secluding squares. Above all, in these one sees the Londoner's alternative to planned urban splendour: he pushes out from his rooms above the merchant's office into the fields, builds square after square all the way from the Charterhouse and Finsbury to Bloomsbury, Marylebone, Bayswater, Kensington and Chelsea; and to the north and south, rather more modestly. To squares he adds terraces, crescents, gardens, places, to the confusion of taxi drivers. One must be struck by the privacy of these places. Almost all are built round a central garden where now the trees are high and beautiful in romantic abandon. For a very large number of them only the inhabitants have the keys that unlock the gates of the gardens in the Victorian iron railings. Only tenants can sit there. The rest of us look down from the top of the bus upon these lavish solitudes, and if we murmur about the selfishness, the stuffiness, the downright cruel snobbery of the idea, we also murmur that it is pleasant to see quiet places and that one might – to quote the familiar London phrase – 'be miles away in the country'. Knock on a door and ask if one can borrow the key and go into the garden and the usual polite, impenetrable London mask is put on and the usual standoffish humbug and evasion begin. The owner 'hasn't got the right' or 'doesn't know who is in charge' or 'who you ought to write to'. (Telephoning is quite out of the question.) There are no phrases that bring a greater look of self-satisfaction to the London public face than 'Closed to the public' or 'We are closed' or 'It is closing time', and you damn the Londoner for his well-fed, carefully put-on air of mild stupidity and vacant pensiveness, copied from the police. Or perhaps the police have copied it from him. And the curse of it is that if you dig back into history, you will discover that he or she is right in a way: when the loveliest squares were built, the fashionable or aristocratic tenants who lived in them dumped all their rubbish and sewage in these places, and there were no gardens at all until the Victorian ironmasters had to do something with all their iron and invented one more wall: the London railing. Gardens do not thrive in mass society. The millions can kill even the London grass. We prefer nature to people. One smiles in despair as one crosses Hanover Square in the summer in the lunch hour and sees only a quarter of the lawn open to the public. The custodians rope off a different corner every day for the office-workers to lie on, while they tend and water the rest. Grass must not get tired.

The square is our characteristic alternative to the *grande place* or the piazza. There are no central places, foreigners complain, where 'Londoners meet' or stroll along together to pass the time of day. The answer to that is, first, that Londoners do not meet, do not gather, and reject the peculiar notion that people like 'running across each other' in public places. They emphatically do not. We are full of clubs, pubs, cliques, coteries, sets, although the influences of mass life are changing us, so that even the London public house is becoming public. But most pubs are still divided into bars, screened and provided with quiet mahogany corners where the like-minded can protect themselves against those of different mind. And – one must admit – with different purses. Clearly, between the saloon bar and the public bar there is, or was, a class division; nowadays, the public bar is where men play darts. In the public bar, there being the thirsty tradition of manual work, you drink your beer by the pint; in the saloon, in the private, you drink it in half-pints; occasionally there is a ladies' bar, and there ladies – always in need of fortifying, for they have been on their 'poor feet' – commonly order stout or 'take' a little gin in a refined medicinal way. The pubs catering for the Irish are rather different; the Irish like to swarm in public melancholy, their ideal being, I suppose, a tiled bar resembling a public lavatory and a mile long, and with barmen who, as they draw your draught stout, keep an eye on you, show their muscles and tacitly offer to throw you out by collar and coat-tail. This is not the London English fashion, which is livelier, yet more judicious, sentimental and moralising. The London publican cultivates a note of moneyed despondency and the art of avoiding 'argument' by discussing the weather. One foggy, snowy morning in a pub in Lamb's Conduit Street, near Gray's Inn, I heard a customer mention the cold and the snow, and, in doing this, he was simply repeating what every customer had said as he came in.

'Couple of cases of sunstroke in the Feobal's Road, I hear,' said the poker-faced old Weller behind the bar – belonging to that generation of Cockneys who pronounced a 'th' as an 'f' and were averse to a final 'd'. He spoke in the gravelly voice of one about to 'cut his bloody froat'.

There are pubs where the same people always meet, where they tell the same stories, where they glance up at the changing London sky and sink into mournful happiness or fatten and redden with natural bawdy – I do not mean dirty – stories but with licence of their own invention. One is reminded that this is the city of the riper passages of Shakespeare and the sexy London papers. London is not puritan; it is respectable – quite another matter. Behind the respectability is the sentimental and fleshly riot. If they can be sure that they are among 'a few pals', the male and female Londoners like to abandon themselves. The whited sepulchres turn rosy, the tongues wag, even raucously sing, and the ladies come out with quiet remarks that are surprising. There is a touch of 'Knees up, Mother Brown' in all of them; in London, Eros is a shade hearty, and what is elsewhere called passion, in London is called being 'friendly'. Friendliness is, of course, double-edged, for it suggests that some would-be friends must be kept out. A little scene I once observed at the bar of the Edinburgh Castle, in

Camden Town – the Bob Cratchit country – goes to the heart of this aspect of London manners. A middle-aged couple were having a friendly talk, and an old man, suffering from city loneliness, occasionally 'passed a remark' – always an offence – hoping to join in. The lady reached for her large handbag – an emblem of respectability – took out a pound note – a sign of grandeur – put it on the bar counter and called to the old man in a 'friendly' voice: 'Have a drink. Say "No, thank you"; I always say "No, thank you" when a stranger offers me a drink.'

And she put her pound note back in her bag, closed it with a slow snap, and, swollen with *savoir-faire* in the art of 'friendliness', she resumed her private conversation. The Londoner knows how to finish things without being, as the saying is, 'nasty'. One had witnessed a death, of course.

And what happens in squares and pubs goes on in clubs, all the thousands of drinking clubs, the luncheon clubs, the dining clubs, the sporting clubs, the dance clubs, to the great clubs around Pall Mall and St James's. You are a Londoner, *ergo* you are a member. You are proposed and seconded; that done, you are among a few friends; you have your home from home. In none of these clubs is any utility or purpose frankly admitted. It is true that Bishops and Fellows of the Royal Society gather at the Athenaeum; actors, publishers and the law at the Garrick; the aristocracy and the top politicians at Boodle's, White's, or Brooks's; that, following

Stevenson and Kipling, a lot of bookish, professorial and civil wits are at the Savile, and professional eminences at the Reform, where Henry James had a bedroom with a spy hole cut in the door so that the servant could see whether the Master was sleeping and refrain from disturbing him. (The hole is still there.) Clubs change. London is made for males and its clubs for males who prefer armchairs to women. The great clubs are in difficulties. Their heyday was the Victorian age, when men did not go home early in the evenings; now at night they are empty of all but a few bachelors, sitting in the dying leather chairs. Some clubs have tried allowing ladies to dine in the evening, but the ladies, after the first rush of curiosity, in which they hoped to find out what happy vices their men were comfortably practising there, tend to be appalled by these mausoleums of inactive masculinity, even when they are elegant, and to be depressed by the gravy-coloured portraits on the walls. The architecture, gratifying to male self-esteem, does nothing for the sex, and the boredom that hangs like old cigar smoke in the air is a sad reminder of the most puzzling thing in the sex war: that men like each other, rather as dogs like each other. The food is dull, but a point the ladies overlook is that the wine is excellent and cheap.

How did this taste for clubs begin? Did it start with the witenagemot or the monasteries? Did it sprout from the guilds – for what are the Drapers', the Fishmongers', the

Armourers', the Watermen's, the Grocers' companies, with their medieval robes and ceremonies, but medieval guilds turned into clubs for the Annual Dinner? The clubs start, as the whole of visible London does, except the Tower and Westminster Abbey, St Bartholomew and the Elizabethan buildings in Staple Inn – the clubs start with the greatest of all London inventions: modern mercantile capitalism. They begin with the coffee houses in the City. 'We now use the word "club",' Pepys wrote, 'for a sodality in a tavern.' Lloyd's was a coffee house, the place where one could read a paper and hear the news, and the more one sat about there, the more one heard. They were often started by servants – the most domineering of men – by the race of Jeeves, for the Woosters, the masters of the world; fashionable clubs like Boodle's, Brooks's, White's take their names from the servants who founded them. The idea has the ease of nature, and it is only in the nineteenth century, when industrial wealth came in, that clubs, like the Public Schools, became outwardly pretentious and exclusive.

And when I say that we have to be members, in the most literal sense the London telephone book is the final guide. There are twenty-eight closely printed columns of other things we belong to, excluding the charities, the social services and the immense network of welfare belonging to the State. The Public Lighting Engineers have their association, God bless them. We protect children in every known condition, animals of all kinds – there is a society for the friends of reptiles – bookmakers, deep-sea fishermen, the industrious poor, amateur weight-lifters; we rally round the most important diseases, from haemophilia to arthritis. The clay-pigeon shooters are united, the pigeon fanciers are international; we visit the indigent blind, convert the Jews and stand by the distressed gentlefolk, New Music, Foreigners in Distress and True Prayer. I say nothing of sects, dogs' homes, cats' homes, girl covenanters and the 'friends' of Bulgaria and every country on earth. One society calls itself simply Nature; nature has to be a member, too.

As for one Londoner meeting another in a public place outdoors, this appears to have difficulties. As I have said, London has no *grande place*. Compared with continental cities, it is poorly provided with places for sitting outside for a chat whenever and wherever you please. A few timid little coffee bars allow one to sit outside nowadays; but there is no stretch of tables on a wide pavement; indeed, one dreads to think of the rows about rights between the General London Council, property owners and the police, who have a mania for objecting to 'obstruction' – a misdemeanour which, like the fog, has no seizable meaning. (It's an 'obstruction' to put up a camera tripod or wheel more than three perambulators abreast in the parks.) Londoners do not like regulations but they adore to moralise about their necessity for someone else. It dates from the Victorian age, when regulations kept the poor in order, and since there is always someone poorer than oneself, the idea of 'the regulations' has become a settled metaphysic. In matters of pleasure, and unlike the French, Londoners have no gift for simplicity. They like their pleasures to be a fuss and an expense – 'the public has got to be protected' – and to be hedged by the objections, refusals, precautions and permissions of the social conscience. One can see that in the 'Naysaying' London face.

After the fixation on property, privacy and order; after the preference for the arguments of the parliamentary to the happiness of the democratic; after our conviction that some of the inalienable right to life, liberty and the pursuit of happiness had better be looked at twice at least; after the guilty feeling that to sit down and just watch the crowd go by for an hour or so for the price of a beer or a cup of tea is idle, bad for trade and that in any case it is rude to stare – would you like people to stare at you? – after all these things, there is the unanswerable climate. It will rain in a minute, and it takes a German Queen Victoria to like picnicking in the rain. And if it doesn't rain, you will be pasted all over with oily grit and smuts. No. Get inside, pay for your drink, finish it quickly. Be considerate – someone else may want the table – go. If you want to sit for hours, go to the parks. In the centre of London you have the largest and most beautiful parks in Europe. Piccadilly Circus is squalid, a comic strip of electric signs at night. Leicester Square has pretty trees, an open garden and a bust of Shakespeare; and people do sit there, packed in a sort of local protest against what London does to the feet in the afternoons. When the evening comes, Londoners traipse round there slowly, six deep. On Sundays, tens of thousands of condemned traipsers dolefully plod round the West End; what else can they do until the cinemas and the pubs open at seven o'clock? It is true that if you listen to the voices on Saturday night you will know that nine-tenths of the crowd are unfortunate foreigners or people from the provincial cities up for the weekend to see the football. I doubt if any Londoner ever sits on the steps round Eros: the crowd watching the lights and the traffic there and filling the chicken and steak bars are Americans, Scandinavians, Germans, French. It is they who scratch messages in their languages on the balustrades of Westminster Bridge; the Germans like to add a literary quotation: 'I have not understood but I have lived. (Goethe).' When Londoner does meet Londoner publicly, the occasion has to be riotous, angry, sporting or royal, in mass condition. He likes to riot on Boat Race night in Piccadilly Circus and, if possible, to climb the statue of Eros and, preferably, damage it. He likes his mass meetings to take place in the one dreadful attempt at grandeur: Trafalgar Square. This place, fouled by thousands of pigeons, washed by fountains that soak the population when the wind catches them and deep in peanut shells, used to be good for nothing except politics. The voices of protesters standing on the plinth of Nelson's Column bounce off the walls of the National Gallery and insult the members of the Government down Whitehall while we stand in the crowd watching the pigeons and looking at the advertisements of shipping companies. They suggest emigration. On Guy Fawkes night and at Elections there is generally a riot here; the teenagers and jackboots are out for the police, and the ambulances carry off those who have been injured by the rockets and jumping crackers. Orgies of victory in 1918 and 1945 took place there. The square is still political, but it has been taken on by tourists and young people, who give it a gaiety that it has not had for a very long time; at four or five in the afternoon, the mass twitter of the starlings kills even the noise of traffic, and the square has its enchanted hour. For these moments of folly London is grateful, but as one looks at the chattering crowds, it strikes one again as typical of the city that they are taking their pleasures standing up.

Orgies of loyalty take place down the Mall outside Buckingham Palace. The crowd is common, free and easy, sometimes rough, but never crazy or hysterical; that was reserved for districts like Notting Hill Gate, for the race riots of fading memory or Wormwood Scrubs, outside the prison when someone was being hanged. Here something dark and ancient issues from the gutters of the city, something atavistic going back to the days of Tyburn Tree and public hangings.

29

Considering that in the eighteenth century London was about the most brutal city in Europe, and in the nineteenth was made savage by the wretchedness of the poor, one is astonished by the calm of manners now, and some say that this repression of native instinct and the general admiration for law and order have led to an increase of anxiety. Yet whenever I come back from abroad, I am always struck by the calm of the London face. It reposes on its worry like a turnip in imperfect soil, and positively fattens on self-control. Of all the capitals or great cities I have known, London is the one least on edge, though often profoundly depressed.

London has the effect of making one feel personally historic; I am not sure why. The rate of change in the modern world is so fast that in a decade we all look like gravestones with half our epitaph written. Yet in its general aspect London is not historic at all. It looks, most of it, like all great cities, comfortably out of date, and the rubbish survives and gets one's affection. Bits of the City date from Wren's time and, after patches of Queen Anne and Georgian, the rest is Victorian, but broken by the new architecture of steel and glass. These buildings have that dramatic air of smashable impermanence which is perhaps the spirit of the twentieth century. But London's traditional weighty permanence and solid planting are deceptive. A large population floats. Millions have not been here for more than a generation; the place is full of Scots, Welsh and Irish, with

Scots predominating, and notoriously they cling together. There is a new population of immigrants from Europe, Africa, Asia, the West Indies. How far back most Londoners go is not very far, except perhaps in the East End and in Bermondsey, south of the river, where the people are long settled and where few provincials have come in. All along the river east of London Bridge the population is clannish and little affected by immigrations. Here, indeed, you catch the jaunty Cockney speech, its whining vowels and ruined consonants, and see the hard-chinned look of indomitable character.

But I mean by the historic sense that personal feeling of background, pattern, and of knowing a lot of things that is common to all Western European cities. London conveys a sense of knowledge and experience. The city works hard but, unlike the Germans, we do not work because we can think of nothing else to do. We are not passionately competitive. We are cautious. We disapprove of the reckless plunge. We like to reflect on our interests. We get no status from self-advertisement. We are economical of means. There are innumerable businesses in London that are run from modest premises and with half the staff of their splendacious opposite numbers abroad, and yet are known to the whole world. It is astonishing that thousands of men can somehow wangle the time to spend an afternoon in the middle of the week at Lord's to watch the cricket – you find clerks, taxi drivers, bosses of companies, salesmen, lawyers, sneaking off for a few hours – for experience suggests that efficiency, being on the spot, and so on often exist merely for their own sakes and are not efficacious. The aggressive go-getter is so often wasting his life and his time pursuing his own shadow. We hate waste. The Londoner believes in timing. This observation had not occurred to me until an artful German explained to me that this was London's key quality. 'You are stupid, but you understand timing and that makes you less stupid, after all, than we are.' The Londoner, he said, seems to be born with this sense. I comfort myself with this compliment when I am enraged by London's muddles, its blank walls, its refusals to move and the dishonest excuses it gives.

But the ageing, the historicising things in London are the dirt, the encrustations of it, and the climate. In three years a new wall of brick or Portland stone is grimed, stained and weathered. Stucco and plaster, which London was fond of, is white today and looks like old cheese in a year; statues get black eyes and weep soot. Metal rusts. I dare not think of what the new glass-and-steel architecture is going to look like at the end of a decade. There are scores of miles of villas in Balham and Clapham, Tottenham and Kilburn, with comic Gothic touches to their bow windows, which already look pinchbeck medieval. Dirt has done it. And on the top of the dirt there is the weather. One can grow years older in the course of a week, often in the course of a day. We are, for example, ten years older since eight o'clock this morning, for we woke up to fog, worried for an hour about whether it would lift, thicken, or – mournful London phrase – 'turn to rain': so often everything has turned to rain. But we saw it melt into feeble sunshine, the temperature rose, a shaggy wind cleared the sky; there was a pause of sunny smokiness and then, over the roofs, we saw white clouds boil up like cauliflowers out of black and thundery pots. What did this portend? Thunder? Gradually light fades. From the top window, we see that South London has gone black. Lights are on in the city. They prick up in our district as the cloud begins to cover us, and there, motionless, it hangs. At three in the afternoon we are living through midnight. What does this mean? Hail? Even snow is not unthinkable; people down our way can remember snow in May. They can remember, giving dates and years, pretty well everything where weather is concerned. The blackness moves off in an hour or so. By tonight we shall be either hot or cold, soaking or gasping, choked or breathing happily, or we shall be – and this is the most likely – living under the dull London lid irritated by a grubby wind blowing off the railway tracks.

Since this is a low damp city the sky means a great deal to us. We are always glancing at it. We notice if the London birds are high or low, quiet or noisy. We get a lot of glum sky, but our general feeling is that just as London generates its fogs, so it creates its own sky – a panoramic statement of the battle between earth and heaven. We get the boiling and racing clouds, we get still terraces of vapour; if the base is brown smoke, the superstructure is often palatial, blinding white, which, in the evening, will be chequered by shadows of violet and saffron. In the autumn the whole show is aslant, riding before the southwest wind; and, except for freak periods of freezing easterly cleanliness in the air, there are long violet hazes in the winter. We do not have those blue skies of the Mediterranean nor those subtle, rippling gradations of blue that miraculously start across the Channel in France, but we have a sudden blue that can be as bold as a sailor's collar, or even lyrical and angelic. Our long sunsets are sad, tender and often melodramatic.

I have just looked out of my window to see if I have been lying. No. In the last half hour a wind has got up, and rain is likely after two days of heat wave – up in the eighties; high for us. It will be a day to spoil picnics in the park, and the lake water will be coldly rippling; but as the clouds move over I can see there are three layers of them on the move, the blue opening and closing between, and I know that if I were flying in over the city I should be looking down on three separate cloud worlds before my eye caught the green city below them. It is June. I shall have to put on a warmer suit. When I go out I had better take an umbrella. And when I do go out I shall think of Constable and Turner, the two great painters of the English sky, and especially of Turner. For it was his painting of the London sky that after a generation came to the notice of the French Impressionists, and over to London they came: Manet, Monet, Pissarro, to get the sky rioting over the brown Thames. It is a satisfactory reflection, for English painting has never stood up to the French or Italian; but we can say, with imperial exaggeration but not total untruth, that the Impressionists 'got a lot from Constable and Turner' and that there is something to be said for our insularity after all.

To the Londoner of my generation, the London sky has another dramatic significance which – once our present boredom with the whole subject is overcome – is memorable. It has been a battlefield. One day in 1940 in the entrance hall of the BBC I heard the sirens howl. One of the maternal ladies at the reception desk called out, 'Air Raid, please' (one is inclined in London to say 'please' for everything, and one must certainly say it out of deference if a VIP like the Angel of Death is announced), but she was in fact telling the boys to close the steel shutters. I shall not forget that large white cloud bellying against the blue in the afternoon and, as my stomach turned over, seeing a flight of silver Spitfires dive into it. I froze with fear, hope, anger, pity. Many times afterwards, Londoners in the blackout heard the sky grunt, grunt, grunt above them, then howl and rock, or saw it go green instead of black, the whole 700 square miles of it twitching like sick electricity and hammered all over by millions of sharp gold sparks as the barrage beat against it like steel against a steel door. The curling magnesium ribbons that came slowly down were a relief to see, in that unremitting noise. The sky shook London like a rug; the floor boards, the furniture, the pictures, the glasses and plates, the curtains, the favourite vases, ferns, clocks, and photographs, the pens on the desks, the ink in the pots danced in their places throughout the night in evil monotony hard to endure. The sky was extravagant; the earth would occasionally come to life in scattered carrotty fires, and on the bad nights, when the docks, the East End and the City were burned out, the tide being too low to give the firemen water, London turned crimson. Even then, people made the 'historic' remark, the remark of experience. Nothing like this, they said, had been seen since 1666. One cloudless August afternoon near the end of the war, green snow fell in minute insulting particles all over Holborn. We saw them when we got up from under our desks, where we had ducked when a bomb had fallen a mile or so away in Hyde Park and had blown the leaves off the trees into these mysterious smithereens. It had seemed, for a moment, like a new venture of the London climate, which we knew to be capable of anything.

Seven hundred thousand dwellings were damaged in the County of London, that is to say more than eighty per cent of the total. And of these, nearly a third were totally destroyed. Little was left of the docks or the City. And about 30,000 people were killed; more than 50,000 injured. On 29 December 1940, all Paternoster Row went, and a favourite phrase, imported from American films, was that 'London can take it', whatever that may mean. London did nothing so exhibitionist, showed none of the characteristics of the prize-fighters' ring, as seen by publicity agents. London was quite simply morose, fatalistic, frightened, depressed, and fell back on that general practicality of mind that counts as calm. The climate had predisposed us to expect the worst and to disbelieve in the facts. Fatalism is the English religion. 'London can take it' is just the beer talking. At the George, in Great Portland Street, I do recall two drunks discussing the kind of funeral they wanted, with a lot of circumstantial detail about the correct amount of flowers, during a bad half hour. And there is no one who could not supply a list of old aunts, grandmothers, and so on who stuck the thing out, immovably, sustained by a vigorous social disapproval of the whole shemozzle. Private life rules the world.

It was the silence of London in the early evening that struck one. One had never known it to be *dead* quiet before. The machine had stopped. One walked down mile after mile of empty streets to the sound of one's own heels only, and voices carried far, as if across water. I remember two painted old crones sitting out alone on a bench in Lincoln's

Inn Fields when I was fire-watching. They were, no doubt, caretakers, and I could hear their voices far across the square. They were talking about actresses and distant connections of the Royal Family, of course. One night I saw a soldier come fighting out of a pub and get his teeth knocked out. One could hear them fall as distinctly as pebbles, a hundred yards away.

It is normal for the square mile – it is really larger than that – called the City to be silent at night. The millions have gone home to their suburban villas to clip their hedges, mow their lawns and admire their roses, and at night one has the impression of being in a medieval citadel, in overpowering stone. Aldersgate, Cloth Fair, Charterhouse, All Hallows, Austin Friars, Bevis Marks, Moorgate, Cornhill, Threadneedle, Cheapside, Eastcheap, Lombard, Crutched Friars and those humbler names – Beer Lane, Bread Street, Pudding Lane, Milk Street, Ironmonger Lane – take one far back. Here modern London really does feel old. Here they dig out the Roman wall and the Roman sculpture and the coins. Here all streets are narrow. They are the original streets and alleys of the Middle Ages, even though all of the blackened buildings are of today. The scores of banks and shipping offices weigh upon the mind, and from their names alone one would know where the mind of this city is: it is, as I have said, abroad. This, one physically feels with a kind of awe, is where the power lies, and the habit of power is deeply founded. Yet even this prison-like place of stone which is ruled by its own magistrates, which employs its own police, with red-and-white-striped bands on their cuffs and with taller helmets, has its gardens, its trees, its green cloisters and shaded graveyards. There is a mulberry tree in the pretty garden hidden behind the Drapers' Hall; plane trees grow before the Custom House. And since 1940, the night walker in the City sees a place made dramatic, bizarre and even frightening by the waste places and gashed cliffs of masonry left by the bombing. The sight is jagged and austere, a place fit for Hamlet's father to walk in under the moon.

London has no style – we repeat – but greed, negligence, muddle, the belief in nature; in short, the dread of plan, the passion of the counting-house for property – and to the merchants property is a sign that the human past is on one's side – have made the accident of nature the alternative to style. And so across the wastes of London Wall, where the bracken and the willow herb grow deep in the ruined cellars, where old safes and the burned-out mattresses of night-watchmen lie, one sees the new glass skyscrapers rise here and there at random, dramatically. A new city which might have been fine to look at is going to be the usual London mixture; rich men and architects without talent are going to be moral about it. Here and there one of the Wren churches will be set off with advantage against the glass houses. Before the wilderness has been rebuilt and the air and space driven out, there is just time to see the City looking strange, fearful, unearthly and moving. It won't last. None of these emotions pays.

The privacies of London, the taste for clubs, membership and coteries must be understood to extend beyond the personal into the markets and sideshows. There is no place in London where one can sit and watch the show go by and, in a sense, the show does not go by but is in hiding; and there is no capital that has such a wealth of peculiar hiding places open to the public.

There are the open markets, entrenched in their traditions and differences. The hats of the Billingsgate fish porters are as notable as their language. Covent Garden is notorious for its feats of hopper-carrying; perhaps from the licentious traditions of Hogarth's days, perhaps from the presence of the Opera House rising out of the smell of vegetable stalls, orange peel and flowers, the tone of this market is loudly musical and amorous. A woman walking through those streets somewhere between the National Sporting Club, the Communist Party Headquarters, the Opera House and Bow Street Police Court is likely to be followed by the more pressing bars of a love song that ends in a heavy crash of crates. Covent Garden is the home of strength. In the afternoon lull, men pass the time punching one another, and youths wrestle on the backs of vans. When a girl passes, they pause as they realise how they are wasting their time and strength, and about that sort of realisation common London puts on a jaunty polish and is not at all shy. Smithfield for meat, Leadenhall for poultry, Bermondsey for hides, Tooley Street for butter and bacon, Southwark for foreign fruit – it is close to the banana wharves. In most districts there are street markets. There is Brewer Street for the foreign cuts of veal, the foreign fish – the octopus and *langouste* – a little London, Paris or Naples, with the snails just flown over and artichokes three times the size of anything we can grow. There is, the most famous market of all, Petticoat Lane, in the Jewish quarter of Aldgate and Shoreditch. Thousands pack into this narrow lane between the sweatshops and bomb sites on Sunday morning, and it is the nearest thing London can offer to an Oriental bazaar without the convenience and cleanliness of the bazaars of, say, Istanbul or Isfahan. They used to say that you could walk through this market and see your own handkerchief for sale on a stall by the time you got to the end – an illusion that dates from the days of *Oliver Twist* and which had vanished thirty years before Dickens started writing about the real thieves' paradise: Saffron Hill. I was brought up on scandals of a similar kind about the dogs sold at the dog market in Bethnal Green; you met your own dear Airedale painted black and offered as a retriever. I am sure this is untrue; the dog market is the most respectable of markets, if a shade shrewd. The real hazard in Petticoat

Lane is of being crushed to death or being deafened by the men and women at the stalls, who have burst their larynxes, destroyed their throats and are down to catarrh and tonsils. The old gags never change. 'Nah then, come closer. What's that? You're not my bloody sister. My family's like me, ugly as hell. I'll tell you what I'll do. Will any lady or gentleman present do me the favah of lending me a pound note?' And so we go to the well-worn London jokes about double beds, cold nights, the 'old man' and the 'lodger', the cheerier kind of smut that London ladies love, especially the elderly ones. You don't walk down Petticoat Lane. You are moved, six deep, in a solid procession of bellies and bottoms – Cockney, Jewish, Negro, Lascar, Chinese. A steamer hoots from the dirty river. Head and shoulders above the crowd will be that pink-feathered Zulu Prince, the racing tipster who calls himself Prince Monolulu, a mobile pursuer of pleasure who can be met any day on the tube between Aldgate and the Tottenham Court Road, making the girls scream with his devouring smile. There will be that glum spectre with his billboard, denouncing the Jews for trading on Sunday morning. He is shoved on, as you are, passing the stalls where they are selling stewed eels by the cup and black-currant cordial by the glass; cockles from the Southend mud, hot dogs, and sugared apples. A yell will come up from your boot. You have almost trodden on a fanatic who has sat down in the middle of the street crying out, as if he were on fire, 'Ladies! Ladies! Nylons penny a pair.' And just when you are so crushed that anyone could strip your clothes off you and you could move on, in perfect decency, stark naked, and nobody notice, the impossible occurs. With a sound of kettledrums, the wheeze of clarinet and trumpet, the boom of a sad slack drum, the blind men's band forces it way through with its one-legged collectors fore and aft raking in the cash. In the right quarters in London everyone knows 'the Lane'. It has its characters, its cliques, its hierarchy. There is a shop in Camden Town with the words 'Cohen of the Lane' on its front – as one might say Lord of the Isles.

There are the junk markets. The Caledonian, now below Tower Bridge, has so gone up in the world that it is now-adays an outdoor branch of the West End shops – at any rate, in everything except second-hand clothes, where sales move fast. There is Portobello Road on Saturdays, the best and oddest market for antiques in London, outside of the great salerooms and the shops of the profound specialists. To go to Portobello Road on the off days is to be treated with suspicion: Are you in the trade? Their last Queen Anne mirror went on Thursday. It is up to you whether you come again. And so on. You understand their attitude: Are you snooping around for someone? Who are you *in* with? They've never seen your face before. 'Are you' – that inevitable standoffish look says to you in a variety of accents that range from Joyce Grenfell's to Sairey Gamp's or from upper-class Cockney to van drivers' rhyming slang – 'are you a "member"?' You go away past the prettily done-up houses of the neighbourhood, skirt the murder area in Notting Hill Gate and pass the new housing estates and fine schools that have sprung up on the bomb sites of one of London's sinister mixed-up quarters, only half a mile from the race riots. But on Saturday you return. The Portobello inhabitants have now put on their act of being local characters, half of them out of Dickens and the other half dreamy connoisseurs. The antique trade of London is tough and intimately connected; it shows a head in innumerable districts; it is a collection of tricky eccentrics, watching one another like spies, and it is the least oncoming, the most misleadingly absent-minded trade in London. And why not? A large number of its clientele – I mean the core of the business, not the casual dropper-in – are obsessed or mad. One was a next door neighbour of mine, a very pretty Irish woman of forty, who collected ecclesiastical rarities and old books. Many times have I helped her carry heavy bundles from the bus stop. In fine weather she put all her finds on the windowsill of her house: candlesticks, missals, royal crowns, a full altar load. She also collected packing cases and newspapers by the thousand, and her diversion was to go out into the garden and change everyone's laundry round, putting Number 2's shirt on Number 3's line and so on, at the same time declaiming that the dirty rotten priests had broken up her marriage to the Duke of Windsor. She was taken away in the end – she screamed so much at night – and what a sight met the dealers who came to her house! One of their van men, wearing a green baize apron, came down the steps wearing a golden crown on his head. She was an extreme case; but one has only to see the glint in the eye of a collector of ephemera to know that it is a trade without quarter, even in its higher courts, like Sotheby's and Christie's, where they are knocking down Italian primitives, a Picasso, a Gainsborough or a Goya. The crowd sits in a little congregation in Christie's room. A well-dressed crowd at chapel, one would say, and the auctioneer knows most of their names, knows what part of the world they come from, what their madnesses are, who or what is between them, who or what is behind them, and is quick as a knife to spot the tactics of the sinful: 'I must ask you, sir, to stop trying to interfere with the bidding.' 'I didn't do anything.' 'You did, sir. You turned round and made a face, sir, three times. Stop it.' You realise in a moment like this that the ease and amusement of the London markets rests on an iron authority.

Diamonds are sold in the street in Hatton Garden; the stock-jobbers pack Throgmorton Street outside the Stock Exchange. Lloyd's conducts itself like a market under cover, not as an office; so do the Baltic and the Wool Exchanges. When I was a youth I marked catalogues in wharves and salerooms. It was a grounding in the deceptive laziness and watchful closeness of London trade. The kind of man they loved to torture was the go-getter, the smart, progressive, pushing fellow. They raised their eyebrows; they handed him the rope, and he soon hanged himself, if he did not reform. Of course, one or two big fish got away; and then, it is worth a lot to see the rosy moral look come on the London face.

The idler sideshows go more lightly. You wake up in some stark American-style service flat in the Edgware Road to the sound of the Horse Guards trotting off to the Palace of Whitehall. I know I ought to know which are the 'Tins' and which are the 'Blues' but I do not. (Not a member.) Any morning in the Mall you will see them. They have the sort of get-up (one hates to admit) that can be seen outside the President's Palace in Lima or, I believe, in the new regiments of Zaire: something between the dress of the Victorian Fire Brigade and an amateur dramatic society's costumes for Gilbert and Sullivan. Still, our fellows are smart and are beautifully in control. At St James's Palace, as the red guards click like toys, you may see a royal and golden coach picking up an ambassador as if he were Prince Charming and not Comrade Yukabolakov or Hulobula, one-time graduate of the London School of Economics, only a year out of a bedsitter in Hampstead and deeply hostile. With luck you may strike a State funeral. Down the street to the single, deadly tap of a muffled drum, the Guards march with arms reversed, like votaries of death in the gloomy bearskins they learned to wear in the Crimean War. The Minute Gun goes off in Hyde Park, and the pigeons in thousands fly off the ledges of the buildings they are ruining. These State shows are good; millions of people slept out on the streets through a night's cold rain for the Coronation. They were, as their lugubrious singing indicated, beside themselves with happiness. Intellectual England sits on the fence and is generally indifferent to Royal show business. There is no doubt that the Monarchy has got the London crowd, and one has only to talk to any London stationmaster, who puts on his top hat when he sees the Royal train off, to know that the sense of being royal is infectious. This is a matter which was gone into splendidly in *Harry Richmond* by George Meredith, who understood the psychological consequences of the cult of royalty very well and enjoyed the comedy. But Meredith was an intellectual.

After Royalty, the best sideshow is that other majesty: the law. Here the London genius has flowered and in soil that (one would have thought) was hostile to blossom. Impossible that the minds of Forsytes, of Dodsons and Foggs could contain such a degree of fancy. Yet they do. The courts of law, rough places like Tower Bridge Police Court, Bow Street – strongly smelling of disinfectant and policemen's hair oil – Quarter Sessions, say, near the Elephant and

Castle, Crime at the Old Bailey, Contention at the Queen's Bench and those strange legal triplets, Probate, Divorce and Admiralty, are dedicated to performance. My own interest began in childhood when I stood at my father's office window in Newgate Street watching the crowd queue up for some murder at the Old Bailey opposite – Crippen, it may have been, or that Mr Pooter from North London who 'did' his Carrie with poisoned chocolates and then sawed her up, one of those quietly thought-out London crimes. There is a definable population of court fans in London. They start the day early at Bow Street to see the prostitutes, the drunks, the small thieves dealt with. You remember the youth who quite preposterously broke an old London custom and stole the pennies people leave on the news-vendors' boxes when they take their paper; for there are two things you can safely leave about anywhere in the open in this city: small change and milk. Both are pretty well sacred. This youth must have come from Liverpool or Glasgow. The thing to do is to stay at Bow Street until the pubs open at 11:30 – there are many comfortable ones near Bow Street, one with a fine collection of theatrical prints – and then, after a beer, to move up to the Old Bailey or the Queen's Bench. There are only about thirty murders a year in London, which makes the place look tame beside Dallas, New York or Chicago; and last year not many more than 300 cases of assault and robbery; burglary and shop-breaking

48

bring out our real talent. Fourteen hundred woundings sound bad, but – to put us in the international picture and the modern world – crime is increasing. We have a special distinction: ten per cent of London births are illegitimate.

In general, it is the quiet and the simple patience of the courts that one notices. Compared with the tribunals in Paris or Naples, compared with what one sees of American courts in the films, the London ones are conducted with a childlike gentleness of tongue. To hear an Old Bailey judge gently extracting the exact position of a dozen hoodlums outside a doorway in the Edgware Road and explaining it all to a jury in words of one syllable is to hear a model of the law's special kind of innocence. I don't say we haven't got prejudiced, ill-tempered, excessively moralising judges, but they are all dabsters at fact and at musing over it. About the alarming aspect of the scene there can be no question. It is at first boring, then startling and impressive. The wig transforms a man, gives him either a death's head, a bibulous joviality or the morbid air of experience in sin; the black robes are severe; the starched bibs are razor-like and elegant; the scarlet-and-ermine robes are womanish and overwhelming. Before speech begins, one is in *Alice in Wonderland*; after it has begun, in that astonishing persistence of Dickens. The air is motionless and tepid. A small cough – caught perhaps in the draughty stone stairways of the Middle Temple or Lincoln's Inn – the turning of the pages of briefs, the moistureless voices of lawyers engaged, as it seems, not in a trial but in an insinuating picking over of chicken bones among educated friends, stiffen behaviour. A very thoughtful game of chess is going on at dictation speed. A pawn – it might be oneself – goes into the box; king's bishop sits down; queen's bishop gets up; a knight scratches under his wig with a pen. Wrapped in his scarlet, the Lord Chief Justice – that untakeable old piece – moves hands that look bloodless.

The law is a tedious profession and it relieves the boredom by its own little comedies. Judges love to tease the police, who go red in the neck; counsel hope to cheer the judge by a little home-made wit. Down at Quarter Sessions near the Elephant and Castle (is that name really a Cockney mispronunciation of the Infanta of Castile?), I heard counsel prosing on. 'And you may think, m'lud, that it is not without significance that when the prisoner signed these cheques he appended the name Ernest Stoney – a reference possibly to the circumstance that he was, at the time in question, without funds!' The judge, like a small juicy sirloin of beef looking out of his regalia, gazed sadly at counsel.

'Not one of your best, Mr So-and-so,' he said.

'An inadvertence, m'lud,' murmured counsel. He was satisfied. The calamities of legal wit have to be borne stoically, like the other sufferings of mankind.

We look across the court at the confidence man who

tricks Colonials in the Strand – the old goldmine story – to the boy killer with the vain smile on his lips, the race-course thug who whines that he was 'only 'aving an ice cream' when the event occurred, the dim little hang-dog chap with forty-seven convictions for theft, the woman empurpled by her uncomprehended load of enmity towards us. In a way, it all sounds so unfair; the law dressed up for its charade, and the rest of us in our navy-blue suits belonging to another world. Until some truculent navy-blue suit goes into the witness box and gives a fine performance in the art of stone-walling learned counsel. The flummery does not conquer the inner London truculence and independence.

Among the sideshows in London must be reckoned the large population of arguers. At lunchtime in the City, at places like Tower Hill or in Lincoln's Inn Fields, they set up their boxes – Communists, Patriots, members of this League or that – and harangue the office workers. It is all done in the parliamentary manner, even when it is irascible. We know the forensic style. At Speakers' Corner near Marble Arch, the affair is hotter, more restive, yet also enlivened by farce. Sunday is the natural day for this fundamental puritan pleasure. Tyburn Tree, the gallows where many Londoners met deserved and undeserved ends, used to stand in the middle of the terrifying traffic there – priests, rebels, high-waymen were hanged here: Fielding's Jonathan Wild, and Jack Sheppard, among them. The last man to be hanged there was the engraver Ryland, to whom Blake's father wanted to apprentice him, but Blake, seeing his face, said, 'It looks as though he will live to be hanged' – which he was, in 1783, for forging bills. This quarter, more than any other, was the gathering place for the London mob, in all its blood-thirsty spirits, right into the nineteenth century. But it has been the place for free speech ever since the Reform Leaguers in 1866 tore up the park railings, scattered the police, and got the right to say what they liked there, in the teeth of the Government. The meetings at Hyde Park are, all the same, decorous, outdoor parliaments alive with heckling and jeering, but in a good-natured way and never as rowdy as some of the scenes in the House of Commons are.

The Londoner loves an argument: it feeds his other pleasure – rumination. He loves anyone who sets himself up as a character, revelling in the vulgarity, the rough, incurable lark of the idea. There are usually a dozen big meetings going on. Last Sunday there was a characteristic London tussle. Lord Russell got up on a box to speak on the demand for unilateral nuclear disarmament and used a microphone. That is illegal. No microphones in the park. You can talk, but you mustn't make a noise! This may sound like a joke, but it is one of those tussles for freedom that always occur in this corner of London; the matter is often trivial, or farcical, the consequences are considerable, and any limitation awakens the Londoner's rage. But, in

52

the main, the standards of Speakers' Corner are low and primitive. There you will meet those earliest manifestations of the dialectic life on earth; the conjunction of two men standing nose to nose, with two or three friends attending, each proving the other wrong, with disparaging, rational calm and pith. ('You say the Buddha is living. How do you know the Buddha is living? Have you seen the Buddha with your own eyes?')

From across the street the shouting under the trees at Marble Arch sounds like a dog show. What are they barking about? Religion, of course, is one subject: Catholics, Protestants, Mohammedans, Orthodox Greeks, Atheists are here tripping one another up. Philosophers appear. 'When I look at you going off to work in the mornings, I'm sorry for you. I'm lying in bed.' Interrupter, 'Who with?' 'Ah, that's another thing, you're sex-starved. No. Not with that lady over there either. As I was saying . . . ' 'Go on, get on with what you was saying,' chants the crowd. And a favourite London cry, 'Where was Moses born?' goes up. Some old gent – I've seen him for years – dribbles on about there being millions of gallons of water up in the sky. 'Where? Up there, Dad?' ask the soldiers who always turn up there on Sundays. There are the Irish, storming away about the men in gaol in Belfast. There are the Communists, arguing with the young. There are men who want the West Indians out, and those who want them in. A lonely figure disputes the

Virgin birth; an elderly man tells us the pyramids hold the key to human destiny. 'When I become Foreign Minister in my country,' some African begins in a soft melting Oxford voice. Insult, doom, destruction are offered all round, and every now and then the little crowds give way to one or two licensed interrupters who are well-known nuisances. 'The logic of history proves . . .' cries a speaker, his voice rising to the high, dead, steel-drilling sound of triumphant rant. But, 'No!' a man shouts from the back of the crowd. An elderly man with his coat open and hat on the back of his head elbows his way in to say, 'What's all this about? What's all this? Come to my office, Number 10 Downing Street.' He is in a temper, grinds his teeth, makes a strange noise like a turkey cock grating its wing on the ground, suddenly stamps in half a dozen frightening steps with all the vanity of a celebrated pest and marches out of the delighted crowd to mess up another meeting.

The speaker begins again. 'The logic of history proves . . . ' What does it prove? Nothing.

And all around, the Guardsmen – fellows who have stamped themselves silly at Buckingham Palace the day before – stand pink with pleasure. Sailors are happy, and the police stand by like hospital nurses, for nurse is never far off in London.

Fights are far less common than they used to be. In Victorian and Edwardian times, they were everyday affairs.

'I told him I'd knock him down.' How often I heard that phrase among my elders when I was a boy. After all, 'Two Lovely Black Eyes' was a favourite song of the Edwardian music hall. But the gangs of Teds, the lads with flick knives and bicycle chains, have grown; dances end in thuggery; there has always been brutality underlying the London mildness. But no one shoots. We think we have that advantage over any other city of this size for a simple reason: our police are not armed. The crowd are usually hostile to the police but they never forgive the man who pulls out a revolver. Violence in London takes on other forms now, generally in random destruction – smashing telephones, lavatories, doors, windows and government property – and deadly motorbicycle tournaments by a new young race of black-jacketed, knife-carrying sado-masochists.

The final sideshow, when one has done the superb museums and art galleries, the cathedrals and churches, the libraries and monuments, the zoo, Hampstead Heath on Bank Holiday, the Cup Final, is the population of eccentrics. We, of course, hardly notice them and never have. Hazlitt said 180 years ago that you could dress up in fantastic clothes or behave in fantastic fashion in the street and not a soul would take any notice of you – on the general ground that it was your business and nobody else's. Our public eccentrics are not exhibitionists, they are not trying to draw a crowd – as has happened often in Paris. They are doing the very opposite: they are – and we understand this – withdrawn deeply into private life. The so-called King of Poland, who, a few years back, was often seen walking barefoot down the Strand in red velvet robes, golden hair down to his waist and a royal wreath on his head, was never gaped at. A bus conductor might wink at another bus conductor or nod his head – but no more; and these acknowledgements expressed pleasure. On the Number 6 going down Edgware Road one sometimes met a merry baggage who carried a spare hat in a brown paper bag and changed it in the bus, singing out, as she did so:

> 'He called me his Popsy Woopsy
> But I don't care.'

And she got out at the Haymarket to dance a little on the pavement if she was in the mood. There is a native rattiness or dottiness among the pavement artists. David Burton – one of the most gifted: 'Gastric and duodenal Pains for 14 years' was the substance of his appeal – used to make war on a rival who had a gramophone and a dog to do his begging for him from the dog-lovers, cat-strokers, duck-feeders, horse-sugarers, bird-lovers of Hampstead and the Finchley Road and would scrawl in large chalk letters on the pavement, 'Worship God not Animals'. Burton had his religious side. He had a natural naive gift. He turned out the Blessed Babe at Christmas and once said to me when I admired it: 'I done the lady all right but I couldn't get the kid.'

Burton was the son of a cab driver. His mother was dead. The father used to leave the house saying to the boy, 'Paint a lake.' The boy painted a circle and filled it in with blue. 'That int a lake,' said the father, giving him a clout, when he came back, and, getting a tin of salmon, he scissored out the fish on the label, gave it a lick, and slapped it on the drawing. 'That's a lake,' said Dad. Not a bad lesson, but Burton always claimed he had been punched and belted into the pavement-artist business against his will.

Burton's oddity was simply more productive than the elegance of the Hampstead tree-slasher, the Negro bird-warbler, the solitaries with imaginary military careers who reel off the record, click their heels, salute, and depart, or the clergyman who, exalted, marches down the street shouting 'It's all in the Book.' One has to distinguish between the mad and the people pursuing a stern individual cause: the elderly lady who arrives in white shorts on a racing bicycle at the British Museum every morning, winter and summer. She is a scholar. In another way so is that taxi driver who answers you in Latin, having, he says, picked it up taking bishops to and from the Athenaeum. Camden Town has its well-known misers. And any decent London club will produce for you among its members men of esoteric habit and information: Sinologists who have never crossed the

Channel, old gentlemen who, by some freak, speak Lithuanian, and others who can be heard having scholarly quarrels, quoting chapter and verse, in a library where, when you nervously open the door, they are by themselves. And the fanatical eccentrics: the peer who always carried a couple of concealed bottles of beer to the Garden Party at Buckingham Palace and lowered them in one of the lakes on a piece of string, so that he could sneak off for a drink when the coast was clear. On – one reflects – what a coast! One has only to search for furnished rooms or to live in board residence to find oneself among peculiar rebels. They are really conformists, conforming steadfastly to something that exists only in their minds. There is the extraordinary host of old ladies with port-wine voices; there were those unshakeable Britannias who used to sit under the glass roof of the Langham Hotel during the Blitz doing the crossword puzzle; those landladies in something like Oriental dress who 'take a little something' in their tea, and have long sad love affairs with overfed dogs and hysterical canaries. London is a zoo.

2

THERE IS NO AGREEMENT about how London began. I incline to the view of Geoffrey of Monmouth, the fantastical Welsh historian, who is quoted in John Stow's *Survay*:

> ... [he] reporteth, that Brute, who was lineally descended from Aeneas, the Son of Venus, about the Year of the World 2855, and 1108 Years before the Nativity of Christ, did build this City near unto the River now called Thames, and named it Troynovant, or Trenovant.

About 1,060 years later, King Lud 'repaired' the city, called it Caire-Lud or Luds Town, and established the gate we still called Ludgate at the west of the City. One likes the word 'repaired'; London has often been patched and improved like an old boot – never planned. According to Stow, it was King Lud's brother who dealt with Caesar in 55 BC. Some say this is poetry and that Caesar marched from the Kent coast into the Thames marsh and found a native market established on a small, sound gravelly hill where the Tower of London now stands. The market exploited the troops, grew very fast, and for the almost 400 years of Roman occupation was a place of great importance. The Romans went; it declined and was worth nothing until the Norman invasion in the eleventh century.

London is a market, has always been a market, and it owes its character to the Thames. When one flies into London from the Low Countries, one sees at a glance what that situation is: the Thames estuary is only a few minutes' flight or a four or five hours' sea-crossing from the mouths of three great continental rivers – the Elbe, the Scheldt and the Rhine; and, by the last two, the traditional trade route from Venice to Amsterdam, the richest seam in Europe, debouches into the North Sea. Opposite these rivers, placed at the crossing of the sea routes, the Thames turned London into a natural entrepôt, and centre for transshipment. At the estuary the river is joined by the Medway, and its safe and tricky harbours were excellent for naval defence and shipbuilding. London has its share with Bristol and Falmouth in the honour of the discoveries and enterprises in the Americas, India, Africa, Australia and the Far East. The Thames, as Kipling grandiloquently but accurately suggested, has known everything.

There is nothing splendid or fine about London's

seaward approaches. The estuary is almost without feature. It closes to five and a half miles at the Nore Light Tower outside the line between Sheerness and Shoeburyness. The sea pilot brings the ship down through Queen's Channel or Princes Channel, the Four Fathoms or comes up to the Swin from the north. Of all the estuaries he knew, Joseph Conrad said this one lacked romantic grandeur and geniality. But, he said in the *Mirror of the Sea*:

> . . . it is wide open, spacious, inviting, hospitable at the first glance, with a strange air of mysteriousness . . . There are no features to this land, no conspicuous, far-famed landmarks for the eye; there is nothing so far down to tell you of the greatest agglomeration of mankind on earth dwelling no more than twenty miles away, where the sun sets in a blaze of colour flaming on a gold background, and the dark, low shores trend towards each other. And in the great silence the deep, faint booming of the big guns being tested at Shoeburyness, hangs about the Nore – a historical spot in the keeping of one of England's appointed guardians.

And where the front line of anti-aircraft batteries shot up at the German raiders in 1940. From the beginning of London's history, from the time of the Romans and the Danes, the estuary is where the raids begin.

In this empty region of marsh and low chalk bluff there is

more sky than earth. The ships creep deeper in, through the hazes of the island. There are days when they stand outside moaning in the fog. Sea fog, river fog, land fog – these are London particularities. If the fog is light, one may still have the sudden, unearthly sight of the tall, rust-brown sails of a sailing barge – some 'bricky', low in the water, surviving the competition of the roads and making for the Essex or Kent brick-fields. These broad canvases rise above a craft that seems to stand still until you just hear the whisper of water at the stern. Not more than half a dozen are left of that fleet which sailed in the pages of W. W. Jacobs's short stories and was skippered, according to him, by men stung by capricious girls, entangled by unconquerable widows, annoyed by ships' boys, and who consoled themselves with beer. Jacobs worked in a Thames wharf when he was young, and no writer knew more than he about the Thames. Episodes from his tales are still enacted in real life. The last time I crossed on the Tilbury ferry, a youngster in the engine room sang a love song triumphantly all the way across, while the rest of the crew clenched their fists, talked of wringing his neck and showed signs of being sick over the side: those paroxysms are pure Jacobs.

Your ship moves in towards the oil stores, the power and gas plants that stand up in the marshes like cathedrals; and if one walks later on along the sea wall, one goes for miles in the east wind past old gunnery ranges and small derelict factories (given up generations ago) or comes upon forgotten lime workings. This marshy wilderness is made for murder. Two bodies have just been found there this week, as I write.

It is not until Gravesend, a neat little Regency town of sparrow-brown houses and Victorian villas, now surrounded by building estates, that the working Thames really begins. The sea pilots drop off, and the river pilots and tugs take over. There are now twenty-three miles of continuous dock and wharf before you on both banks of a stream only 700 yards wide here; at London Bridge, it will be only 250. There is an old fort in midstream at Gravesend, and this was the first point at which London could be defended against the Norse raiders. They got in easily. They settled. They brought the word 'hythe' with them: the names of pretty little Greenhithe and Rotherhithe, the church of St James Garlickhithe (where the spices essential to medieval life were unloaded) commemorate them. The sea pilot drops off and reports, no doubt, to the officer known as Ruler of Pilots on the pier there, a title without definite article, as if to say he were Ruler of Heaven and Earth. And in this one gets an insight into the politics of the river, its ancient jealousies, its obdurately defended rights, for the Thames is just as closely tied up in cliques, coteries, clubs and privacies as anything else in London. Ruler occupies a den in the row of green-painted offices on the pier, where Lloyd's' agent sits too, a place that smells of bicycles and tea. The interests of the river are jealous and vested. No one is going to give up a tittle of what he has won centuries ago. He stands by a tradition not for love of the past, but because that is where his bread and butter lie. The Port of London Authority may rule the Thames up to the tidal limit far inland at Teddington, but it has to respect rights that date from the time of the hard-headed medieval guilds. It has to endure the existence of the Elder Brethren of Trinity House, the Guild, Fraternity or Brotherhood of the Most Glorious Undivided Trinity and of St Clement, founded by Henry VIII in 1514. Sea and river pilotage, the buoying of the Thames, the fixed lighthouses between Gravesend and Galleon's Reach – that filthy stretch of water – and the lighting and buoying of a good part of the coasts of England and Wales are the tasks, the privileges of the Elder Brethren. They have their buttons sewn on tight.

One goes up-river now enclosed in noise and caught up in work. This is a working river. Hour after hour the radio-telephone is cackling on the tugs. 'Calling *Sun 17*, take the *Florian* and go in with her. Calling *Sun 16*, has that little Spaniard moved yet? What's the matter with her?' Language, old river hands complain, has become politer on the river. Education, they say, is the curse of everything, and the bad-language joke, refined to a high polish of London irony by the characters of W. W. Jacobs ('The langwidge 'e see fit to use was a'most as much as I could answer'), has lost

64

its anchorage. The *Florian* is one of the ships lying under the tall sky in the sweep of Gravesend water. It bears down like a hotel upon the tug, and the tug's cabin boy brings up the eternal mug of strong tea on which working London lives. If you were to go with him to the dock gate, you would see the beauty of the skipper's job. You would understand why there is all that clever waltzing and pulling this way and that, all that threshing at the stern of the tug as it gently but decisively takes 15,000 tons round a series of sharp right-angle turns into the lock and the alleyways of a dock basin, without touching a quay or any other craft by so much as a graze. These skippers are artists: they bolt down a mutton chop between crises, ruin their digestions, grouse because fog in the estuary has kept them on duty for forty-eight hours without a wink of sleep; but they play their game with the wind, the strong Thames tide, the current and the heavy traffic.

Twenty-three miles of industrial racket, twenty-three miles of cement works, paper-mills, power stations, dock basins, cranes and conveyors shattering to the ear. From now on, no silence. In the bar at the Clarendon Royal, at Gravesend, once a house built for a duke's mistress, it is all talk of up-anchoring, and everyone has one eye on the ships going down as the ebb begins, at the rate of two a minute. The tugs blaspheme. One lives in an orchestra of chuggings, whinings, the clanking and croaking of anchors, the spinning of winches, the fizz of steam, and all kinds of shovellings, rattlings and whistlings, broken once in a while by a loud human voice shouting an unprintable word. Opposite are the liners like hotels, waiting to go to Africa, India, the Far East; down come all the traders of Europe and all the flags from Finland to Japan. You take in lungfuls of coal smoke and diesel fume; the docks and wharves send out stenches in clouds across the water: gusts of raw timber, coal gas, camphor, and the gluey, sickly reek of bulk sugar. The Thames smells of goods: of hides, the muttonish reek of wool, the heady odour of hops, the sharp smell of packing-cases, of fish, frozen meat, bananas from Tenerife, bacon from Scandinavia. Before us are ugly places with ancient names where the streets are packed with clownish Cockneys and West Indian immigrants, the traffic heavy. Some of them on the north side between Tilbury and Bethnal Green are slums, dismal, derelict, bombed; some of them so transformed since 1940 by fine building that places with bad names – Ratcliff Highway and Limehouse Causeway and Wapping – are now respectable and even elegant. The old East End has a good deal been replaced by a welfare city since 1946. We pass Poplar, Stepney, Shadwell, Deptford, Woolwich, the Isle of Dogs – where Charles II kept his spaniels – and now mostly dock, with the ships' bows sticking over the black dock walls and over the streets. We pass Cuckold's Point, where one of the kings of England gratified a loyal innkeeper by seducing his wife. Until the sixteenth century – according to the delightful Stow, who said he 'knew not the fancy for it' – a pair of horns stood on a pole there, a coarse Thames-side warning, perhaps, of the hazards that lie between wind and water.

The Thames, we realise, was for centuries London's only East to West road or, at any rate, the safest, quickest and most convenient way that joined the two cities, one swelling out from the Tower and the other from Westminster. And there is another important matter. It is hard now to believe it as we go past these miles of wharves and the low-built areas of dockland where one place now runs into another in a string of bus routes, but this mess was once royal. The superb Naval College at Greenwich is the only reminder. It is built on the site of the Palace of Placentia, where Henry VIII, the great Elizabeth, and Mary were born. Here was the scene of the luxurious Tudor pageants, the banquetings that went on for weeks, the great wrestling bouts, the tournaments, the displays of archery. It is from 'the manor of East Greenwich' and not from Westminster that the charters to Virginia and New Jersey were given in the seventeenth century. It is odd that London began as a collection of manors and that the word 'manor' is still thieves' slang for 'London'. At Deptford, nearby, was the Royal Naval Dockyard where all the Tudor ships were built – Drake's *Golden Hind* was laid down here. One can see the reason. It is not simply that the Tudors liked building palaces, just as the aristocracy liked building mansions that vied with those of the kings. It is not simply that English monarchs have been a restless lot, although that is true, too. The plain reality is that a monarch who has been churched at Westminster needs money; he has to get it from the City; the City gets it from ships and trade, and that trade and its ports must be defended by navies. Deptford and Greenwich were close to London's fortune, where the goods came in, whence the adventurers sailed, and where the attackers attacked.

The Thames is a main road. It is our Grand Canal, and if you half close your eyes at the Pool, the brown warehouses look like palaces in a smoky Venice. The river men have always quarrelled with the City, and nowadays the quarrel is with the roads, for road transport is killing the coastwise traffic. Some say that in fifty years half the area will revert to what it once was: a pleasure ground, and, heaven knows, the warehousemen and wharfingers of London have up to now killed the waterside as a place of pleasure and amusement. Tug skippers growl when they pass the wharves of the Ford plant at Dagenham, where the iron ore is being grabbed out of lighters, swung high and sent by conveyors to the furnaces, where it turns into red liquid and where the liquid turns into cars and trucks. 'It comes in by water and goes out on wheels,' they say. They hate wheels, for wheels are the enemy of water. But, in London, in England generally, nothing is ever given up if it has a point of law attached to it. The docks were built because the mass of shipping in the Pool became impenetrable; but the lightermen and wharfingers fought for their rights, as hard as Defoe fought for the Dissenters, as the City fought against the King, as Wilkes fought for the press, as the early trades unionists fought. The lighters can be loaded on the water side of the ship, free of dock dues. There is usually money at the bottom of London liberties: there has been nothing abstract in the London view of the desirable life.

The lighters are the craft that distinguish the Thames from foreign streams. They lie like beetles on the water, bring a blackness to the brown of the river and constant change to the jigsaw map of the water surface. Heavy and lumpish, they are moved by the score and are settled in low archipelagoes and islands that will be here today and gone tomorrow, dissolving and re-forming. These masses might be mistaken for derelicts or some fatal stagnation of the river trade; but it is the commonest sight of the river to see a tug rush up to one of these islands, like a dog in a temper; a dozen men jump off; in a few wild minutes the solid block is split into pieces and in a quarter of an hour most of it has gone and the tug is towing a double row of these blind hulks behind her. They never sheer or get out of line in tow; they pass under the tricky arches of the bridges and dodge other packs with the ease of skaters. Their loads are peculiar:

above Twickenham, while you are drinking a glass of beer under the trees at one of the prettiest of the river inns, the London Apprentice, with its Italianate ceiling, the barges unload not only coal for the gas works, but talcum powder from Holland.

These barges are mostly 'dumb': they have no engine in them. One of the grotesque sights of the Thames is to see a single barge, adrift and askew on the tide, with one or two men in the stern, steering with their long oars. Their job looks hopeless. The lump looks as though it will foul all traffic and blunder into the piers of any bridge in its way. But the Thames waterman has not just tumbled into his job. He is no amateur. He has been apprenticed to the use of the Thames tide; he has had to earn his licence.

The waterman was the bus driver and taxi driver of London. The whole population went by river. Kings and queens went up to the palaces at the Tower of Greenwich by barge. Shakespeare's Globe was on the south bank between London Bridge and Blackfriars; the actors and the theatre crowds went 'over the water' – a phrase still used in London life – by wherry. When the roads became safe and coach and carriages came in, the London watermen were powerful enough to hold up the granting of carriage licences for more than a generation. The Thames is marked by 'stairs' and 'gates' where the wherries picked up their passengers. Hundreds still exist: Wapping Old Stairs, for example, and the stairs at London Bridge where Nancy took the boat in *Oliver Twist*. The Royal barges, graceful gondolas in green and red with gilded cabins, lie in the museum at Greenwich. The day of the ferrying waterman as distinct from the lighterman is done, but the old Watermen's and Lightermen's Company, founded in the sixteenth century to stop the perpetual rows about fares, still licenses the apprentices for the Port of London Authority. The old trick of the watermen was not to tell the passenger his fare until he was in the middle of the river, where he was at their mercy. The pretty Georgian building of the Watermen's and Lightermen's Company, its little eighteenth-century face jammed between the fish warehouses in Billingsgate, has a portrait of one of its masters whose lonely distinction it was to be called 'The Honest Waterman'. A matter for astonishment, till the River Police were started at the end of the eighteenth century. At Wapping Police Station, the Inspector claims they are the first police force in the world.

The watermen had a remarkable doggerel poet and scribbler, John Taylor, who in the early sixteen hundreds takes us to the heart of the old Thames quarrel. Actors were a trouble to wherrymen. I shall have to annotate the text:

I myself have often met with a roaring boy [Taylor writes in his pamphlet *The Waterman's Suit Concerning Players*], or one of the cursed crew that hath nothing about him but a satin outside to cover his knavery, and that none of his neither, witness his mercer and his tailor: yet this gallant must be shipped in a pair of oars at least: but his gay 'slop' [his baggy Elizabethan breeches] hath no sooner kissed the cushions, but with a volley of new coined oaths newly brought from Hell to the Bermudas [the 'Bermudas' is thieves' slang for alleys] – like the filthy Straights of Covent Garden [hence the metaphor to be in 'dire straits'] – by the ghost of the Knight of the Post [a sharper]. He hath never left roaring 'Row, row, row, a pox on you row' as if his pink [a harlot] – should stay too long for his pestiferous person and when his scurviness is landed where he pleases, he hath told me I must wait on him and he will return to me presently, and I shall carry him back again, and be paid altogether: they have I attended five or six hours like John-a-Noakes for nothing, for my cheating shark having neither money nor honesty hath never come to me, but took some other pair of stairs and in the same fashion cozened another waterman for his boat hire.

It is not surprising that watermen waited until they got to the middle of the river before tackling some of their customers. And all you had to do on a foggy night, a modern Thames inspector said to me one day, was to give your opponent a faint nudge and over he went, no one the wiser. See the river scenes in *Our Mutual Friend*. But in fact watermen and actors celebrated their uneasy alliance in a sporting fashion, for London unites in sport. One Thomas Doggett, an actor, founded a prize called Doggett's Coat and Badge in 1715 for an annual rowing race of Thames watermen, and it has been rowed every year since. Originally rowed in wherries, it is now rowed in gigs from the site of the Old Swan, near London Bridge, to Cadogan Pier, at Chelsea, and it is said to be the oldest and longest rowing race in the world, the course being four miles seven furlongs. The prize is a brilliant red coat of the period with a large silver badge on the arm, bearing the white horse of Hanover. The vainglorious piece of apparel can be seen in the hall of the Watermen's and Lightermen's Company at the bottom of St Mary at Hill, and there, drinking your ritual glass of sherry at eleven with the courteous gentlemen who are up to their necks in the Thames shipping trades, you can consider the portraits of past masters going back centuries, the lovely Adam ceiling and chimney piece of the court, the remarkable clock, which was once stolen, and other treasures of the ancient Thames from days when it was not quite as respectable as it has since become. There is even a large modern painting of the post-war ceremony with the latest Doggett winner in the foreground and, among the crowd of notables, Eleanor Roosevelt. One of the Doggett winners was an old prize-fighter, Jack Broughton, known as the Father of British Boxing and the first to 'introduce the gloves'.

The docks break up this east London into grimy little Venices. How do you imagine the Isle of Dogs? It is a collection of high, black prison walls and streets without feature. There are rows of small houses, and then, over a dock wall, appears in huge white letters the startling single word *Philosopher*, or some other just as strange. You are looking at the name of a ship whose black bow overhangs the wall of the graving dock, dwarfing trains, buses, houses, everything. Between the new blocks of flats that have gone up since dockland was burned out during the Blitz rise the funnels and the masts; one is surprised to see ships, lightly domesticated, careless-looking, gay and trim, rising with the clean paint of the sea among London's dirty brick. There are havens on the Isle of Dogs, such as The Gun, one of the few remaining public houses with a terrace on the river, where on summer nights one looks at the river and its cold lights and listens to the clatter of the chains and conveyors of industry; and where one waits for that peremptory, half-melancholy, half-majestic sound of a ship blowing as she silently glides out black in the night, almost through the pub yard, from the dock basin on her voyage. 'Nice boys. Very nice fellers they were. And spent a lot of money,' says the woman at the bar, looking towards the sound of the ship she cannot see. There will be no sing-song at the piano in the river room with that lot now. They have gone.

The destruction on the Isle of Dogs during the war was terrible, and no one could get the inhabitants to move. It is true of all the other dockland neighbourhoods: Stepney, Limehouse, Poplar, Wapping, Deptford, Woolwich and Rotherhithe. The river people are as closed to the outside world as villagers, and as tenacious. They are clannish. Warehousemen use a lot of chalk and write jokes on the walls. At a first-floor 'gap' where the crane swings the bales into the warehouse, a wit announces 'Ladies Welcomed'. Someone has clumsily spelled out on a pub wall, 'Lean here not on my van. I haven't paid the instalment', for leaning is a mass habit in this quarter. Dockland politics are hot. The London docker does not want a steady wage, whatever his wife may say: he wants a high wage for a day or two, gallons to drink, and then to rage against casual labour. I have heard dock leaders say the docks are a 'real education, as good as any university'. This clannish sharp population are a variation of pure Cockney. They have grown out of a rich and roguish past in which honest work went on beside the piracy and the pilfering enjoyed by gangs, subtly divided into river pirates, night plunderers, light horsemen, heavy horsemen, scuffle-hunters and mud-larks. They are intensely respectable now and speak piously of the amount of thieving and murder on the Thames in the days before the docks were built in the nineteenth century; the docks and the River Police brought crime slowly to an end, or nearly so. You hear modern tales of ambitious rogues making off with a lighter of copper and modest ones collaring a few cans of tinned rabbit. And Poplar lately has warmed up. Prostitution has started up there in a big way. But Limehouse Causeway has no opium dens; it is a collection of modern flats – one, I believe, is called Bethlehem! The little Chinese restaurants are still in West India Dock Road. You will notice Ming Street. Wapping High Street is a mile or more of wharves and warehouses where you duck under the cranes and hear the warehouseman's old chant: 'Lower. Lower a bit', and see him bring out his double hook to catch the bales. If there is hardly a dwelling house in the street, there is a handsome region of apartment houses just off it. The Turk's Head was bombed. The pretty Prospect of Whitby has become modish. It is the same over the river in Bill Sikes's Rother-hithe. Paradise Street is still an alley, but I don't suppose they ever sing there now:

'You robbed every tailor and you've skinned every sailor,
But you won't be walking Paradise Street no more'

which I have heard London sailors sing in Liverpool, but have never seen printed. There is The Angel, in Cherry Garden Street, where Pepys used to gather cherries when all this was countryside, which has been done up.

Close by is the shady churchyard of St Mary the Virgin,

opposite a little pub called the Mayflower and a street called Clark's Orchard. It was named after John Clarke, who was married and baptised in the church. And who was John Clarke? 'It has long been known locally' – so, in a sublime phrase that shows one of London's villages raising its head, runs the booklet given to me one evening by the landlord of the pub – 'It has long been known locally that it was the Rotherhithe *Mayflower* that carried the Pilgrims over the Atlantic yet facts accepted in a district are sometimes unknown elsewhere.' John Clarke was second in command of the *Mayflower* on that voyage. Christopher Jones, the commander, also lies in this churchyard. He witnessed the will of William Mullins, one of the passengers. It was the first will drawn in New England.

The Three Jolly Caulkers by the Surrey Docks at Deptford commemorates the site if not the house of Dickens's Three Jolly Fellowship Porters. The past of the whole region lives on in street names, with their whiff of sea life: Dock Head, Muscovy Street, Cathay Street, Pickle Herring Street and Shad Thames: there is Free Trade Wharf going back to the river wars.

The walled docks of London are like the great walled demesnes and estates of country gentlemen in the eighteenth century, but the livestock is made of steel; they are, that is to say, like little nations in themselves. Ships look enormous in them. The gates are portentous and, architecturally, are sometimes fine; inside, the geometric scene of basin and warehouse and railway track is spacious – often too spacious and desert-like, for dockland was almost totally destroyed in the Blitz.

One has passed Execution Dock, where pirates were left to hang until three tides had passed over them. One has passed under Tower Bridge. It is London's river gate, the first bridge over the river.

I have said that London has no great vistas, no monuments to mark a beginning and an end, in some way spectacular. Yet, between Tower Bridge and the Houses of Parliament at Westminster, the sight is one of crowded, spired importance. There is a jumble of dignities, there are gestures of grace. Here is individuality, moneyed, pushing, often ugly, sometimes fine; here reposing in classical decorum, there bursting with purse-proud romance – the whole not as clean as it was when Wordsworth stood on Westminster Bridge and not as filthy as it was when Taine sickened at the sight of the dripping soot on Somerset House: London is a little cleaner to look at than it was fifty years ago.

Tower Bridge and Westminster bracket London. The bridge is not ancient. It is exuberantly Victorian – into that matter we will go later on – for the bridge was not finished until 1894. It became, with the Houses of Parliament, the symbol of the city, the image presented to the world, and one of the few conscious attempts to give the flat place a touch of skyline, one of the many wild attempts at London style. The Londoner has always been a suggestible man, the mongrel of history and geography who has been convinced, from time to time, that he is a little French, a little German, a little Italian, and even considerably Greek, and that he is living at any period of history that comes into his head. And so, asked to build an epoch-making suspension bridge that shall be drawbridge as well, he builds – in the nineteenth century – something like a medieval castle of granite, makes its towers look like a cross between a pair of Baptist chapels and Rhineland fortresses, spreads it massively across sky and water, and, at the peak point of London's power and modernity, he creates a bridge suitable for King Arthur, the Black Prince, the archers of Agincourt and the operators of the culverin; in order, one supposes, to disguise from himself the fact that he has really built a masterpiece of engineering. The giant bascules of the bridge weigh 1,000 tons, which can be raised to let a ship pass in a minute and a half. This occurs more than a dozen times a day and has indeed occurred about 325,000 times, without a single failure, since the contraption was built.

In some moods one feels the whole thing is some owlish and baronial fake from a German barony; in others, it has that unhappy familiar ugliness for which we begin to have an affectionate pity, reflecting that it has what in his literary way really the Londoner likes most: character. People put up with Queen Victoria because she had that: something preposterous and incurable. In yet another mood we recover the generous feeling that familiarity and the weather make the bridge part of nature; and, as I have said before, in the best and the worst sense of the idea, we are infatuated with nature. London has the art of looking mysteriously sad. Seen in the kindness of fog or mist, the Tower Bridge has the beauty of a heavy web hung from the sky or floating like some ghostly schooner just above the surface of the water. On clear days, the sky stares through it like an imprisoned face; and, in the evening, if you are sitting on the terrace of one of those little seventeenth-century houses, close to the Mayflower in Rotherhithe, the bridge looks spacious and sweeping, springing lightly over the river, which here is wide. The towers and their cantilevers blacken against the evening sky and, if the sky is feathery or the sunset light and yellowish, the bridge is a noble frame for the pigeon-coloured lanterns and belfries of Wren's churches and the dome of St Paul's, resting, dumb as an egg, on its hill.

A tug with steam up has stood by Tower Bridge for sixty-seven years to help any ship that fouls the piers. Only three times has help ever been required. But the tug stands there by statute, and I suppose always will, while the ship's boy makes tea all day long, for the city that created Lloyd's and insurance is about the most insured place on earth. The duty to keep that tug there will turn, in due time, I suppose, into some privilege that someone will have: the inalienable right to hold a floating tea garden there, almost in the fairway, with a badge of office, a place in the Watermen's Court, even a seat in the House of Lords!

But the builders of the Tower Bridge were influenced not only by the medieval dream. They wanted a construction that would not grossly conflict in style with that early piece of military engineering the Tower of London, which stands by it. This formidable jigsaw of moat, walls, screens, curtains, towers and ramparts is the largest surviving medieval fortress in Europe. It was built by William the Conqueror to cow the City and grew more elaborate as king followed king. It is a citadel with a king's palace and court in flushed brick in the centre – that winey brick, like the blood royal itself, that looks so rich and post-prandial in England, as if it had been copied from the cheeks of Henry VIII. Here are the pleasant velvety lawns over which the great ravens stalk and squawk like dilapidated Tudors. These deadly birds parade like familiars around what, one feels, might be a satisfaction to them: the executioner's block. Ringing the centre is the maze of stone, a stone that is as grey and cruel as frost in a wicked season. There is no grimmer sight in England than this terrible building; the women's prison at Holloway is child's play compared with this horror. For centuries it was the national slaughterhouse, but more frightening to us, no doubt, than to the long

81

procession of famous men who went there to be imprisoned for years, to be poisoned, strangled, drowned, tortured and decapitated, for they were used to Death walking beside them in their short lives and their religion celebrated suffering.

The Tower is now for thousands of schoolchildren and tourists queuing up six deep at the ticket office most days of the year to get their portion of glamorised history which still pours from the Victorian cornucopia. The place has become a fancy of childhood and, also, among adults the occasion for defensive low comedy: the word 'bloody' in English is a blasphemy and always causes rollicking laughter. All Londoners get a peculiar satisfaction out of saying 'the Bloody Tower', the sort of satisfaction Queen Victoria got out of calling Mary I 'my Bloody ancestor' at a Balmoral dinner party.

I find no glamour in the Tower. It appals. The one beautiful thing in it, the small bare chapel of St John, which is one of the finest pieces of early Norman architecture in England, strips technicolour history from the mind. In this bare chapel, the stern spirit of Norman England encloses the mind. The austerity is cold yet elating. Suddenly one understands the humility of the medieval soul, its violence and its terrors. A figure like Richard III is native to a place like this, and Shakespeare's histories become comprehensible when one has had one's soul hardened by the fortress and prison that surround this small yet powerful Norman core.

All European cities have these lumps of dead history in them; they obstruct the mind, lie inertly across it for centuries and do no more than alert the fancy for an hour or two in those happy times when a sense of the past is a personal taste, a passing wonder before which we congratulate ourselves on our progress or, at any rate, on our change. But a real sense of the past cannot exist without a sense of the present. We are now closer to the Middle Ages than the Victorians were. These picturesque lumps bristle and wake up. In what way does the medieval ethos now differ from that of Europe or, indeed, the greater part of the world? The Tower means murder *now*, torture *now*, stranglings, treacheries, massacre, the solitary cell, the kick of the policeman's boot. The scratchings on the walls of the Tower are the scratchings of Auschwitz. We are reminded of what the words 'struggle for power' mean in our own age. It may have astonished Victorians that Wren's uncle, a harmless, dull and climbing bishop, was shut up here for eighteen years; but that sort of thing does not astonish us today. It is normal. I say nothing of the Great. The Tower, grey and nasty, is awake again, and the dirty water of the Thames lapping under Traitors' Gate, where they rowed the fellows in, looks sly and has the light of a conniving modern eye.

And yet the Tower was never as formidable as it looks.

It was built, as I have said, by William the Conqueror to overawe the City, but accident and the illogic of life in England made the plan ineffectual at once. The centre of Monarchy and rule had always been in Westminster and Whitehall, a long way off. The Tower could not protect Westminster, as Trevelyan says, from the insults of the London mob. Rebels got into it. In Queen Anne's time it was no more than an arsenal; it contained the Mint, and although occasionally a prison, it began to serve as a zoo and a museum of armoury and kept a stock of lions and other wild animals.

We have passed miles of cranes, forty-six miles of them, to be exact, if we reckon both banks of the river. They are thickest in the Pool, like an infestation of grasshoppers sticking an articulated limb, with an insect's unknowable intention, into the sky. One waits, like an entomologist, for one of these lean creatures to move a leg, a feeler, a proboscis, to bend the tip of an antenna; and then for it to drop a bale into a lighter, dead straight and suddenly, like a spit. Pedantic, doctoral, these insects are: they hiss as they act. At London Bridge they suddenly thin out. By Blackfriars they have vanished. Trading London ends; ruling London begins. Or, rather, the historic market gives way to something new. We have travelled to the limits of old London. We have seen the ball flaming like a head of golden hair on top of Wren's Monument, the Doric column that marks where the Fire began in 1666 and destroyed almost all Elizabethan London that had lasted until that time, the destruction that cleared the ground for a modern city. London Bridge is the divide.

And the Londoner's mind splits also, as T. S. Eliot divined when he wrote *The Waste Land*. Over the bridge, evening and morning, the city clerks march ten abreast to and from their offices in regiments brought in by the suburban trains.

Unreal City,
Under the brown fog of a winter dawn,
A crowd flowed over London Bridge, so many,
I had not thought death had undone so many.
Sighs, short and infrequent, were exhaled,
And each man fixed his eyes before his feet.
Flowed up the hill and down King William Street,
To where Saint Mary Woolnoth kept the hours
With a dead sound on the final stroke of nine.
There I saw one I knew, and stopped him, crying:
                                      'Stetson!
You who were with me in the ships at Mylae!
That corpse you planted last year in your garden,
Has it begun to sprout? Will it bloom this year?
Or has the sudden frost disturbed its bed?
Oh keep the Dog far hence, that's friend to men,
Or with his nails he'll dig it up again!
You! hypocrite lecteur! – mon semblable, – mon frère!'

Yes, all bookish men, though many only of the book-keeping kind. The corpse they bury in their suburban garden is a self, one of their several selves: the one that catches the train and sits under the green lamp or the fluorescent light in the stony daylight of Lombard Street, working on documents from Hong Kong or Sydney, listening to the mash-mash-mash of computers. The riper and older this corpse of his, the better his roses at Dulwich or Blackheath, at Croydon or Kent House or Hammersmith.

The Bridge was called 'the absurd old bridge'. Tall houses stood on it unsteadily for 650 years. Pepys saw it burn: 'an infinite great fire'. The maid woke him up to see it. The bridge was deadly to navigators, and some of its arches used to be jammed with the bodies of dead starlings; the birds have nowadays moved westward with civilisation to Trafalgar Square. The old houses came down in 1750; the present bridge, dusty in the summer, windy and bleak in the winter, was built in 1831. It has one fine building on the northern side – Fishmongers' Hall – and one lovely church below it in Billingsgate – St Magnus the Martyr.

The southern side of London is crossed by miles of high, bowling, blackened railway arches, solid as Roman walls, deeply tunnelled and cellared, never penetrated, I believe, by bombs. If London were totally devastated, this would, very likely, be the only surviving architecture of the city, outlasting all, as the Roman aqueducts have done in Spain and Italy. The arches converge rumbling on the bridge and on that steep cobbled hill rising out of the Boro' where half a dozen times a day the dray horses used to go down defeated when I was a boy. And here the Londoner's mind splits into past and present. Every street name takes a bit of him into a past he cannot but know. At London Bridge he knows he is Chaucerian, for the Canterbury Pilgrims started off only a few hundred yards away; he knows he is Elizabethan; he knows when he goes down to the wharves of Bankside that Chaucer's father sold wine on the quay opposite; he knows Shakespeare took the wherry across to get to the Mermaid off Cheapside or to his lodgings near Houndsditch. There is not a vestige of it all to be seen; only the names remain. The sight of those names is strange and dramatic. Bankside was the quarter of Elizabethan bear gardens, theatres, taverns, wrestling grounds, brothels. The place was a fairground. Paris Garden: the name evokes something other than the present glum street of printing works and factories, of lorries loaded with bales of paper. You go down there at night and the alleys around Bankside are empty, the warehouse doors are bolted, the black walls are cut sharply at corners and against the sky, the cranes are still. There is only the dry, dusty, cold after-smell of trade, and the sound of the river, a rustle that grows to a loud flopping, as if a great dirty carpet were being shaken from bank to bank, when a tug goes by. There is a pub down there, and you can sit on the heavy river wall and look across to the lit-up dome of St Paul's and the office blocks opposite, in one of those stretches of city peace that are moving because of their emptiness. Like some promiscuous jade, some bedraggled old Madame wiping the gin off her lips, London has wiped out half of its history. The Chaucerians, the Elizabethans might be another race; Elizabethan England lives only in the country; almost all of Elizabethan London was destroyed in 1666.

Between London Bridge and Blackfriars on the south bank, and, on the north, as far as the Strand, we break with that time. We know how much a Warwickshire man Shake-speare was, but how much of a Londoner was he? Typical, in one sense: he was not born in the city. He arrived from the provinces, as tens of thousands still do, to be part of the floating, the unsettled, rootless population; there is evidence that he stuck to lodgings for 'single gentlemen' for many years. He may have been one of John Taylor's 'roaring boys' in satin, uttering 'new coined oaths' to the wherrymen. London life was river life, but he never bothered to mention it. Having made money, he did as Londoners do: he moved 'out' and bought a 'place' in the country. We are told by historians that all London was singing ballads and reciting poems at this time, glad to be rid of a Spanish King, an ailing Papist Queen and religious persecution. The fires of the martyrs were out in Smithfield, and London was jolly: so gay, indeed, that the belief is that since Elizabethan times London character has changed and greyed over. The balance of character may have changed. It is as dangerous to judge a people's character by their literature and their art as it is to look at art and literature without consideration of people and the times. There had been Puritans in Langland's time, their moralistic strain deriving from social rancour. But in Shakespeare's days English imagination and moral energy had been assuaged by the open Bible and the pox had not yet spread its sadness. Shakespeare is Londoner enough in his gravity, his quick wits and his absorption in human nature. He quickly picked up the sea-going patriotism, but, perhaps because the Monarchy had the patronage, he does not show much esteem for the City except for its taverns; only in *The Merchant of Venice* does he crack up the Rialto-going class and the City privileges. And the merchant city of Venice is the one city of Europe that most resembled London in condition. The Mayor and Aldermen in *Richard the Third* are comic hobbledehoys – a matter that may show Shakespeare shared the aristocratic class prejudices of his time – although he gives them the credit for remaining silent in disapproval of Richard's kingship. It all came from Holinshed, of course, and perhaps Shakespeare did not care. But he did care for kings and princes, the supreme form of the new individual the Renaissance had released. Great cities do not live in a vacuum. They live in concert with other great cities. London was great because Amsterdam and Paris, Milan, Rome and Venice were great. London was simply the last, the most westerly city of that chain which runs from Constantinople, Athens, Venice, Paris and the Rhine. Constantinople falls, the classical revival begins, the Renaissance glorifies Italy; very late, the awakening reaches London, and it is to Italy and the classics that the rough, extravagant English turn; Chaucer and Shakespeare are Italianate. Elizabethan literature catches the sunflash of the Continent. It finds a focus, subjects, a style. And it is a stroke of luck that in being the last recipient of the Renaissance, London should be splendidly placed by geography and natural gift for the new inspiration of the age of discovery, with its incitement to extremes, to adventure, fortune to all that lies outside the small glass panes of the Elizabethan manor. For centuries London had lived in the expensive delusion that it was French or that France belonged to it; that was done with. Londoners were free of that, free of the centralising Papacy; they were on the edge of the Atlantic itself.

We know what the age of discovery did for Elizabethan drama from Marlowe's *Tamburlaine*:

> Look here, my boys; see what a world of ground
> Lies westward from the midst of Cancer's line,
> Unto the rising of this earthly globe;
> Whereas the sun, declining from our sight,

Begins the day with our Antipodes!
And shall I die, and this unconquerèd?
Lo, here, my sons, are all the golden mines,
Inestimable drugs and precious stones,
More worth than Asia and the world beside;
And from the Antarctic Pole eastward behold
As much more land, which never was descried,
Wherein are rocks of pearl that shine as bright
As all the lamps that beautify the sky!
And shall I die, and this unconquerèd?
Here, lovely boys; what death forbids my life,
That let your lives command in spite of death.

Men are sought

    ... whose faculties can comprehend
The wondrous architecture of the world,
And measure every wandering planet's course,
Still climbing after knowledge infinite,
And always moving as the restless spheres
Wills us to wear ourselves, and never rest ...

So Shakespeare's heroes are put to the extreme test. Language itself is young. The times are not reported by Shakespeare, they exist by refraction in his images.

Everything before them seems old, especially the language. Suddenly it breaks from the Latin chains. Verve, exhibitionism, native personality burst through. Thomas Nashe has the local London voice:

Let me see, hath any bodie in Yarmouth heard of Leander and Hero, of whom divine Musaeus sung, and a diviner Muse than him, Kit Marlow? Two faithful lovers they were, as every apprentice in Paul's churchyard will tell you for your love and sell you for your money. The one dwelt at Abidos in Asia, which was Leander; the other, which was Hero, his Mistress or Delia, at Seslos, in Europe, and shewn a pretty pinekany and Venus priest; and but an arm of the sea divided them, it divided them and divided them not, for over that arm of the sea could be made a long arm. In that division rested, and their towns that like Yarmouth and Lowestoft were still at wrig wrag, and sucked from their mothers' teats serpentine hatred one against the other. Which drove Leander where he durst not deal above aboard, to be seen aboard any ship, to sail to his Lady dear, to play the didopper and ducking water spaniel to swim to her, not that in the day, but by owl-light.

Until the waves 'gave him his bellyful of fish-broth' and served up his parboiled corpse for Hero's 'dejeune or breakfast'.

The Reformation is done with, the religious wars are over and – very nearly – the religious persecutions. The monasteries are gone. A prudent Queen, mean because her father has ruined the currency, manages, blows hot and cold like a double-dealer, is all for reconciliation, profit and subtlety. The new, shot-up nobility intend to keep their political spoils. It is a period when London must have been full of the ruthless, new-rich: ostentatious, energetic, piratic, treacherous, hard, greedy, out for adventure, released for danger, superficial, educated, cunning, pious, and, as the age closed, melancholy. They were surprised, as they went to the block, that the amazing show had been deceitful and fortune elusive. We read Sir Walter Raleigh's words:

> Tell fortune of her blindness;
> > Tell nature of decay;
> Tell friendship of unkindness;
> > Tell justice of delay;
> > And if they will reply,
> > Then give them all the lie.

We pass after London Bridge from the London that made the money to the London that ruled, to the region crowned by what Rose Macaulay in her book on Milton called the Englishman's particular vanity: his political conscience. If Church and Throne had been in the City instead of in Westminster, would the English have developed those three outstanding traits: their love of liberty, their predilection for hypocrisy and their romantic snobbery? (The last goes back a long way. Platter, a Swiss who came to London and who wrote in 1599, counted thirty skulls of traitors on spikes at London Bridge and was astonished to hear people loudly boast that they were the skulls of their relations, all of noble family.) The nobility and the lawyers moved westward; the former building palaces now gone, the lawyers – many of noble family – were already in the Inns. Shakespeare must have gone to Gray's Inn in 1594 when *The Comedy of Errors* was given for Queen Elizabeth and the lawyers drank a toast to her, which they do once a year still. It is strange that although London wipes out its past, the Londoner does not quite forget, though he may not quite know what he is remembering. When I was a boy, we prayed every morning at school for the soul of Alleyn, who was called by Ben Jonson the greatest actor of his time. He put his money into country property and founded the school. The ghost of Alleyn presides over one of the wealthiest slices of suburban property in London. The men vanish, but toasts, prayers – and property – remain.

3

WHEN DOES MODERN London begin? When do we begin to recognise a house, a large building, a conversable Londoner? The Elizabethan age is imaginable; it is inflamed by literature and it is recorded in histories; but, put among the Elizabethans, we would be bewildered and frightened aliens. The crowds in Smithfield, the worshippers in one of London's oldest, loveliest of churches, St Bartholomew the Great, the fantastic crowd of tumblers, mountebanks, quacks, thieves, whores and traders at Bartholomew Fair, the theatre-going, bear-baiting crowd in Bankside, the poets of the Mermaid are as foreign to us as the crowds of an Asiatic bazaar. When we see the disorder of India, we are looking at what London must have looked like. The words and actions of the Elizabethans may fill our minds, but their context and their persons are as strange to us as Cathay was to them.

It is not until the middle of the seventeenth century, when

the ages of prose and sobriety start, that recognition begins. First there is the Civil War, when the grace of the Cavalier and the sternness of the Roundhead begin in opposition but end by producing a London blend which is neither one nor the other. Milton sits in a room in the Palace of Whitehall that Cromwell's troops have looted, writing despatches in Latin, and is no Puritan:

Because you have thrown off your Prelate Lord,
    And with stiff Vows renounced his Liturgy,
    To seize the widowed whore Plurality
    From them whose sin ye envied, not abhorred,
Dare ye for this adjure the Civil Sword
    To force our Consciences that Christ set free,
    And ride us with a classic Hierarchy
    Taught ye by mere A. S. and Rutherford? . . .
    But we do hope to find out all your tricks,
    Your plots and packing worse than those of Trent,
That so the Parliament
May with their wholesome and preventive Shears
Clip your Phylacteries, though baulk your Ears,
And succour our just Fears
When they shall read this clearly in your charge
New *Presbyter* is but Old *Priest* writ Large.

In 1940 many in London turned their memories to the lines of Milton's *Areopagitica*, for danger does not kill

96

our passion for dispute. Milton wrote when his London was in danger:

First, when a City shall be as it were besieg'd and blockt about, her navigable river infested, inroads and incursions round, defiance and battell oft rumour'd to be marching up ev'n to her walls and suburb trenches; that then the people, or the greater part, more than at other times, wholly tak'n up with the study of the highest and most important matters to be reform'd, should be disputing, reasoning, reading, inventing, discoursing, even to a rarity and admiration, things not before discourst or writt'n of, argues at first a singular good will, contentednesse and confidence in your prudent foresight, and safe government, Lords and Commons; and from thence derives itself to a gallant bravery and well grounded contempt of their enemies . . .

It was a century of war, disasters and wonders. In 1665 and 1666 there was the Plague, the year of 'Throw Out Your Dead!' when 100,000 died. Foreigners who came to London to see the richest city in Europe were appalled by the filth and inconvenience in which Londoners lived. The island that has so often been the first in manufacture, trade, craft, political long-headedness and united patriotism has usually been slow to change its customs. The floors of palaces and great houses were still covered with a compost of rushes, new layers being laid on old and the human and animal stink alleviated by a top dressing of rose leaves and lavender. Carpets and panelling to replace the cloth hangings had not come in, so that floors and walls were infested by the plague-carrying fleas of the black rat. Two generations would pass before the uninfested brown rat destroyed the last medieval black rat and London became free of the sickness.

The Fire followed the Plague, and it is after that disaster that the London we can see and the Londoner we can know and talk with truly begins. All the City went up in flames that blew in the east wind up Fleet Street and the Strand as far as Whitehall and northwards into Holborn. People threw their goods into boats on the Thames. The poor did nothing to stop the Fire at first; the rich refused to allow their houses to be blown up in order to make a break the flames could not leap across. John Evelyn wrote:

Oh, the miserable and calamitous spectacle! such as haply the world had not seen since the foundation of it, nor can be outdone till the universal conflagration thereof. All the sky was of a fiery aspect, like the top of a burning oven, and the light seen above forty miles round-about for many nights. God grant mine eyes may never behold the like, who now saw above 10,000 houses all in one flame! The noise and cracking and thunder of the impetuous flames was like a hideous storm. The clouds

also of smoke were dismal, and reached, upon com-
putation, near fifty miles in length. Thus, I left it this
afternoon burning, a resemblance of Sodom, or the
last day.

The Bible-reading Londoner, apocalyptical, liable to see the
Wrath, had emerged.

Some years later, the mild Thames froze up for weeks,
an event unheard of for centuries, a thing fantastic and
phenomenal. Londoners moved out onto the ice, opened
shops and roasting booths, theatres, bull-baiting shows,
brothels, and organised horse-coach races, even set up
a printing press. Evelyn walked across the ice from Westminster to Lambeth and dined with the Archbishop; in
miniature, London put its life on ice.

By now the burned-out City was being rebuilt. Even
London fogs date from this time, for St Paul's was built out
of the tax on sea-coal brought down from Newcastle, and
the records are full of complaints about the new poisoning
smoke. In its new brick from the Essex brick-fields and its
scaffolding, London must have looked something like old
Warsaw being rebuilt in the Fifties. It was being designed
by new men under the eye of one of our brilliant, dissolute,
art-loving kings, whom the Puritans have loathed and the
mass of Londoners loved. Charles II had known in his exile
what it was to be hungry. He had lived in a Paris garret. He

had mixed with the crowd. Who were the new men? Some of them, with Christopher Wren at their head, led the scientific awakening that had spread across Europe under the name of experimental philosophy. They belonged to the recently founded Royal Society. It was housed in a building sold to them by Nicholas Barebone, the son of the rabid 'Praise-God' Barebone, who had given his name to Cromwell's Parliament. The younger Barebone was a speculating builder, making money out of unplanned and shoddy buildings after the Fire, especially in the regions of Chancery Lane, lawyers' land. He was very representative of those whose outcry killed Wren's plan for giving London the classical magnificence of Paris, Venice, Milan or Rome. If London is wiped out again, the first voice that will be heard after the calamity – if any is left – will be the voice of a London ground landlord screaming for his property like Shylock for his ducats and his daughter. As the lower kind of Puritan business man, Barebone can have had nothing in common with Wren, who was a gentleman, the nephew of that bishop who served eighteen years in the Tower for his ardent Royalist sympathies, an intellectual, and a scientist of genius. Wren is London's 'miraculous youth'. He was fitted by a superb, delightful brain and great vitality to great tasks. He worked day and night, as the saying is, until he was ninety, and all his work was experiment and invention.

Court patronage ceased when the Civil War came, and

Inigo Jones, the Surveyor of Royal Buildings, was dismissed and violently persecuted by the Puritans, who hated art as much as they hated the King. They hated churches and palaces; architecture died. The centre of intellectual life moved to Royalist Oxford. Until Court patronage came back with Charles II, Wren was an astronomer. The Restoration was his stroke of fortune. There is an account of the awkward meeting between Cromwell and Wren as a young man. 'Your uncle,' said Cromwell, 'has long been in the Tower.' 'He has so, sir,' Wren replied, 'but bears his afflictions with great patience and resignation.' 'He may come out if he will.' 'Will your Highness permit me to tell him this from your own mouth?' 'Yes, you may.' But the old Bishop had the family tenacity: this was not the first time, he said, he 'had received the like intimation from that miscreant'. He 'disdained the terms projected for his enlargement which were to be a mean acknowledgment of his favour, and an abject submission to his detestable tyranny'.

Wren was a prodigy. When patronage gave him the task of rebuilding the City churches after the Fire – besides St Paul's, eighty-six had been burned, and he rebuilt or superintended the rebuilding of fifty-one of them – he set about the task with the gifts of the geometrician and experimental engineer; it remained for the aesthetic imagination to be awakened. Once more in the visual arts we see

101

the importance of London's fertilisation by the Continent. The aristocracy and the rich merchants had only to go to Paris or to Venice – the city they had by now replaced as the centre of European trade – to see a magnificent city and noble buildings. It was not that the British lacked genius in design; Inigo Jones, who was the son of a London cloth-worker, had no fame in England until he became famous in Venice and in Denmark. What was lacking in London was opportunity; that existed only in the country, where the aristocracy preferred to live. Wren's genius as an artist did not awaken until he went to Paris and saw Bernini building the Louvre, but that experience was decisive.

It is often said in criticism of Wren that he was a scientist before he was an artist; and if this is so, we can only say that such an impurity is native to the British. Wren's art was a delight in new and ingenious practical experiments and the pursuit of individuality. Each of his churches is different. New architectural problems are proposed – new kinds of nave and roof, every variety of lantern and spire. One can pick out twelve different kinds of tower in his churches, and in the interiors the same original, various, exploring spirit is at work, a spirit enchanted by its own cleverness. Yet Wren is not an English eccentric. He was grounded in principles; he was exhaustively thorough. His reports show him to be both daring and practical, voracious for activity. He had grown up discreetly in a revolution. His churches were to be designed for Protestants. The galleries which he introduced are a requirement of the Protestant service, where all participate, but his domes and cupolas have the intellectual gaiety and adventurous spirit of the Catholic and Baroque.

The churches were for merchants who were men of this world and who liked a display of wealth and condition. They would reject a plan for rebuilding the City because it interfered with freeholds; but, as in their City companies, they liked to display their possessions: carving, plate and inscriptions. Wren cared for these things too; he was often paid in plate. In discussing London pride and the anomalies of English character, one notices that if some failure of the larger visual imagination so often occurs out of laziness, compromise and self-sufficiency, it is a character liable to the lyrical, to sudden originality and the response to style.

If Wren is more scientist than artist, his work has the lightness and intelligence of art. At Greenwich, where he followed Inigo Jones, at Chelsea, at Hampton Court, he gave London its finest things. His spires give the City its notes of elegance, that Caroline grace and body which are sensuous, intelligible and serene. Nineteen of his churches were destroyed in the Blitz, two of them outside the limits of 'the square mile', the City of London: St Clement Danes (Dr Johnson's church) and St James's, Piccadilly, but they are now restored. The beautiful tower at St Mary-le-Bow, in Cheapside, has been rebuilt; also St Stephen, in Walbrook, which Dr Nikolaus Pevsner – by far the most instructed guide to London's architecture – calls the most majestic of Wren's parish churches. For myself, it is the loveliest classical building in London. Not all the fine churches are Wren's – the extraordinary church of St Mary Woolnoth, at the corner of Lombard Street, for example, is by Nicholas Hawksmoor, of his school – but in them all one understands there was a core of gold in the mercantile and moralising mind of seventeenth-century London, and that it is a founding quality. Again and again, it reappears in London's history.

From the memorials on the walls of these churches, the tablets, the urns, the busts, one has insights into the individual character of the citizens. Not God, one would say, but human nature, the history of families, the signal character are being worshipped here. A society commends itself as it also commemorates. The notion is Protestant: this is not a faith inspired by the humility of saints, but of men and women who insist, as a rising class, on their position when the last trump shall sound. They are independent, purse-proud, notable. Whether their destination is hell or heaven, they will lead the dutiful procession and with a due sense of rank. The inscriptions are often worldly, but we must not forget that this was the age when the Royal Society declared for simplicity, precision of language and the observation of fact.

At St Dunstan in the West, the tablet to James Chandler,

banker and Sheriff of the City of London reports his virtues briefly but states that 'he was very beneficent to his Relations to whom He parted with £20,000 in his life time'. The words 'parted with' have a ring of the counting-house. There is a plaque to Edward Lloyd, the founder of maritime insurance, in St Mary Woolnoth's; and in that small, strange Baroque church with its white fluted pillars grouped in threes, its gilded Corinthian capitals and its lovely black carving, a church that is more like the antechamber to a palace or the court room of one of the old guilds or livery companies than a place of worship, there is a tablet which gives a cry of conscience. The merchants and adventurers were subject to remorse: here, John Newton, clerk, once 'infidel and libertine and servant of slaves in Africa', proclaims his redemption. At St Bartholomew the Great a mariner of the Revolutionary period tells in doggerel the sufferings he underwent as he fought and traded in the Levant for the decent support of his wife and children. And, now and then, figures less trite in expression appear. At St Dunstan in the West, again, there is the tablet to Alexander Layton, 'Fam'd Swordsman':

> His thrusts like lightening flew, more skilful Death
> Parried 'em all, and beat him out of Breath.

The imagination and minds of the Elizabethans were directed, as we saw, beyond themselves to the discoveries of new lands and new lives. In their reflections about themselves they show little curiosity: they know their lives are brief, their fortunes uncertain, and their very sense of the uncertainty of fortune gives them a pride in having little to say about themselves. After the Revolution and with the arrival of experimental philosophy, the mind becomes practical and curiosity turns to self-discovery and to what is here and now in life. These new people are in at the birth of bourgeois society and they are basically like ourselves, except in one respect: they do not shelter, as we have come to do, in a general urban anonymity.

One sees these men appear in the book of the man who invented biography: Aubrey's *Brief Lives*. Nothing of the Plutarchian or classical essay; nothing of literature. Aubrey is a botaniser among his contemporaries, a gossip collecting facts, an experimental philosopher compiling his catalogue. We pick out a man like Dr William Harvey, the author of *Essay on the Motion of the Heart and the Blood*, who told Lord Bacon that he wrote philosophy like a Chancellor. 'I have cured him,' Harvey said. Aubrey adds each fact like a specimen. Harvey thought best in the dark, he notes, and built caves in the earth under his house so that he could meditate. To cure his gout, 'he would then sitt with his legges bare, if it were frost, on the leads of Cockaine house, putt them into a payle of water, till he was almost dead with cold, and betake himselfe to his stove, and so 'twas gonne'.

His famous book ruined his practice. Harvey was a man of genius who said that men were no more than mischievous baboons. Aubrey collects his facts at random.

A character like James Bovey brings us closer to the London merchant. Bovey was born in Mincing Lane. He was sent in boyhood to learn languages along the trade route and returned to be a bank cashier, then traded on his own account and retired to write a book called *Active Philosophy* which contained a list of 'all the Arts and Tricks practised in Negotiation, and how they were to be ballanced by counter-prudentiall rules' and a 'Table of all the Exchanges in Europe'. Habits: very litigious, poor stomach, lived on chicken, could not get on with red-haired men. Aubrey goes on:

> From 14 he had a candle burning by him all night, with pen, inke, and paper, to write downe thoughts as they came into his head; that so he might not loose a thought.

Like a decent London merchant, he spoke 'High Dutch, Low Dutch, French, Italian, Spanish, Lingua Franca and Latin'.

But it is Pepys who is the model in whom we recognise a near contemporary. His background is the perennial London background – his father came up from the country. The family had well-connected cousins but the father was poor, and when he came to London at the age of fourteen he was a tailor's apprentice. One gets a glimpse of the City struggle. Pepys, the elder, was a 'foreign' tailor, that is, not being London-born he was kept out of the powerful Merchant Taylors' Guild and worked on his own. His right to do so was doubtful. The act was piratical. Industrious men in his situation were Puritans from necessity – many were beginning to emigrate – and the tailor, who had married an ignorant laundry maid, kept his doors shut on the temptations of the town. His mind was formed by the Bible; to the rowdiness of the Elizabethan taverns, to the dancing, finery, card-playing, fighting and wenching, the Pepys family opposed the disciplines of work and respectability. When the younger Pepys was a boy and stood in the crowd to see Charles I executed, he rejoiced at the defeat of evil. The only signs of backsliding in Samuel Pepys were his secret expeditions to the theatres at Bankside and his love of young girls; and, when he became a man, the spell of London adapted him to its life. For although London was for the Parliament and against the King who had robbed its tills, it was quickly sick of the Civil War and wanted to get back to its business. The Puritan strain in English character is only a strain and is most intimately concerned with economic disadvantage, more with the private war of the rising man or class with the settled and rich, when these try to stifle him, than with the theology of Calvin, who seriously thought it desirable to make a totally new and just society. Calvinism was logical and continental; only the Scots found it congenial. Illogical Londoners compounded with the society provided for them but fought inch by inch for their economic, religious and political freedoms within it. They were patchers in mind as they were in building.

Pepys was more than willing to compound with London. He would go to church, he would listen to Presbyterian sermons, he put business and industry first, he was conscientious, he made money, he was far too cautious to get into trouble. He was a first-class civil servant. But he liked wine, plays and women. He spoke with the King. There is nothing rigid or dry in him; he is warm-hearted but he is not profligate; for although his complaints of the libertinage of Charles II's Court have a touch of sneaking humbug in them, they also veil a romantic aspiration as well as expressing a genuine fear for the government of the nation. Whatever is said for Puritanism or against it, one effect seems to be constant, and perhaps it is the most important: it gave the individual a dramatic inner life and an acute consciousness of the self. The effect of a Puritan upbringing upon a man of Pepys's temperament was to awaken his curiosity about himself and the times he lived in. He saw life minutely as something novel. Some secretiveness of nature – for the Puritans were no friends to the heart when they indulged their senses – and, also, his justified fear of death, for he suffered from the stone all his life, must also have created the diarist. (The magnifying glass had come in, as a toy, and Pepys soon got one; he did his best to save it once when he was attacked by highwaymen.) He delighted in his magnifying glass, whether it was applied to a louse or to his person; and some of the scientific spirit of the age that created the Royal Society trickled down to him from intellectual men.

Such influences played a part in producing a new kind of man: the curious enquirer, the recorder of the ordinary world. Pepys has been called the man who saved the British Navy at a time when it was in decay and danger, an administrator of the highest kind, dogged, persistent and indefatigable; but his novelty lies in his excited, fearful, amiable, busy interest in Thomas Gray's 'pleasing, anxious being', and in the day he is living in. The heroic age of London had gone, as surely as the age of chivalry had gone in the Spain of Cervantes; a spirit more observant and sagacious replaced it.

The struggle of Pepys's father with the Guild or Mistery of the Merchant Taylors is an incident in London's painful transition from a medieval economy to capitalism. Through-out medieval Europe all trades were organised into guilds, and men had by law to belong to them. They embody the pre-capitalist system when there was no master-servant relationship in trade. A man was apprenticed, served his time, became a freeman of his city and, by election, one of the officers of his guild. In London the guilds absorbed the whole political power of the City and their wealth was immense. The most powerful of these were the Goldsmiths, incorporated in the early fourteenth century under the title of the Wardens and Commonalty of the Mistery of Gold-smiths of the City of London, and they have to this day their Hall on the original site in Foster Lane. The decline of the guilds began when they fell into the control of their rich members, who were often simply merchants and not craftsmen, and sometimes not of the craft at all; they became early capitalist corporations, and the poorer men had to fight against them. The power of the Goldsmiths lay in their control of coinage and valuables; they fulfilled the role of bankers and safeguarders of moneys before banks were invented; and in fact when the Bank of England was founded in the early eighteenth century the Goldsmiths violently opposed the innovation and with some success. (They ingeniously organised a run on the Bank.) And it was the City companies who resisted the terms of King Charles I, a refusal crucial to the course of the Civil War. It is characteristic of the London temper that the guilds have not vanished although on the Continent they vanished long ago. London never gives up an institution, though it may exist simply as a ghost. Their existence is shadowy: their great wealth is in property, and from it they now support charities and famous schools and give sumptuous dinners in their palatial halls. Those built before 1830 are very fine, particularly Fishmongers' Hall and the Hall of the Goldsmiths. The Goldsmiths still have an important function. They have the obligation to assay all gold and silver in Britain, and their 'hallmark' – literally the mark of their Hall – is not only an international standard of quality and purity, but has passed as a metaphor into the language. At Foster Lane, one can see them any day putting their mark upon the English wedding ring. At the end of his term, an apprentice is still expected to submit a 'masterpiece' of craftsmanship in gold and silver, as his forebears have done since 1607. And the Company have the duty at the ceremony called the Trial of the Pyx to test the gold and silver coins of imperial currency issued by the Mint.

When Pepys was wakened by the maid to see London Bridge on fire, another Puritan only five years old, and living in St Giles, Cripplegate, has told us that he was watching the same sight. It is a lie. It has been doubted whether Defoe remembered either the Plague or the Fire, for his parents had probably taken him to the country for safety. But Defoe is an important variant of the Puritan spirit; if Pepys is acquiescent, Defoe is the rebel fighting on his own. Defoe's forebears, also, came up from the country. His father was a poor tallow chandler, one of the lowest of the City trades; he was glad to better himself by turning butcher, just as the son eventually bettered himself by adding an aristocratic 'de' to his name. Defoe, like Pepys, came of a severely pious family who had the same Puritan passion for education and money-making; the same common sense, but an aggressive inheritance. If Puritanism gave people an inner life, it may be said that, in Defoe, this amounted to not much more than an hysterical fear of the Devil and a shopkeeper's sense of right and wrong as a crude matter of debit and credit; but, in fact, the effect of Puritanism on Defoe was also to make him discover a self that could be dramatised and saleable. Like Pepys, he is totally concerned with recording the domestic life of his times. He brings home to us an age when London felt itself to be young, not old, as new as its new brick. But as he does so, it is in the interests of his own advancement and the advancement of others.

Defoe is not the first picaresque writer to come out of London: Chaucer and the Elizabethan Nashe precede him. But it is Defoe alone who can most interestingly be put beside Gil Blas or even Lazarillo de Tormes, and when we see them together we see the irony of the difference between the new capitalist Europe which London led and the Europe that was still courtly or feudal. In Spain, the picaro is a rogue, the unemployed starving student in a society still dominated by the Court and where no rising middle class exists; he can be only a servant; in England, where the Middle Ages are dead and capitalism is establishing itself, the rogue is the

Puritan. He is a man on his own account. His adventures tend to success; his misadventures to endless sermons and pages of advice. Defoe – like Barebone, the speculative builder – is an operator; he is the first vocal businessman deep in speculation, lawsuits, trickeries, full of ideas for doing business and making a quick fortune. He dealt in hosiery, wine, oysters and bricks. Only one of these ideas strikes one as being sound, and it seems to have been his stand-by in many troubles: the brick and tile making. London clay made excellent bricks; the demands of the growing city after the Fire were enormous, and by setting up at Tilbury he interposed himself between his Dutch competitors and the market by saving on shipping charges. The bricks were certainly delivered on the cheap sailing barges of the Thames. After his years as a hosier in Fore Street – to this day the rag and haberdashery trades still have their warehouses in Fore Street and Cloth Fair, close to St Bartholomew the Great and Smithfield (which is still London's meat market) – Defoe went bankrupt and turned to journalism and politics. (He went broke for £17,000, an enormous sum in those days, and, like a circumspect Puritan, paid most of it back.) A born pamphleteer, he attacked at the top and made himself the terror of bishops. It was part of the old war between the middle-class City and ecclesiastical, aristocratic and monarchic Whitehall; when he was put in the pillory the London crowd were on his side, for he knew the London crowd inside out and spoke in their dogged, common, good-natured voice. He had an art pretty common in London, which may be called the art of relentlessly keeping one's temper. But he was also a humbug, a realist who knew on which side his bread was buttered. He was, of course, the first sensational journalist, exploiting his crime or sex story and covering it all up by putting on moral airs. His gentlemanly contemporaries thought him low, ill-educated and unpolished; the last was certainly true. He was as plain as a yard of cloth. But his fight to get to Whitehall succeeded. He became an intimate of William III. He sat with Ministers of State. He also discerned the character of the English of his time when he created Robinson Crusoe: an adventurous, self-possessed, practical pioneer and colonist knocking up a gimcrack colony on a desert island. And in doing this, like a good Puritan with a theatrical mind, he did not object to the suggestion that Robinson Crusoe might be an allegory of the harassed and ambiguous life of Daniel Defoe, shipwrecked and alone on the desert island of Great Britain. His body lies among the jostling ranks of the tombstones in Bunhill Fields. On a silent City night one can cross the acres of bomb site where the bracken grows and pass to where the glass-and-steel buildings of the new City rise above the ruins of a City whose manners Defoe delighted in, and stand beside the graveyard where he lies. The scene is ghostly, for there is a suggestion

115

of solid complacency in the faces of those large white illegible stones, jammed together as if to embody the whole spirit of cantankerous competition that Defoe and his new London lived by:

> A true bred merchant [Defoe said] is a universal scholar. His learning excels the mere scholar in Greek and Latin, as much as that does the illiterate person that cannot read or write. He understands languages without books, geography without maps; his journals and trading voyages delineate the world, his foreign exchanges, protests and procrastinations speak all tongues, he sits in his counting house and converses with all nations and keeps up the most exquisite and extensive part of human society in a universal correspondence.

The age of projects, plans, coffee houses, newspapers, Lloyd's insurance, the joint-stock companies had set in. London was becoming stoutly middle-class, sensible, insistent on guarantees, a place, above all, for conversation. The English novel was founded. The ideal man was the man of the world. Men of 'wit and distinction' talked with 'women of discretion'. The lines of Pope proclaim the London mind:

> . . . presume not God to scan;
> The proper study of mankind is man.

116

There was not an ugly building in London, Horace Walpole said. This was not quite true, but the new parts had that sedateness and domestic dignity which were to last until the full shock of the Industrial Revolution was felt. When one tries to imagine Londoners of the eighteenth century, the age of Fielding, Richardson, Johnson, Boswell, Dryden, Pope, Hogarth, Reynolds and Gainsborough, one is struck by the fact that they are, by taste, urban. They are men of fashion, politeness, wit and the town. Their feeling for nature, so strong in Englishmen, is a townsman's feeling; the sort of nature admired by the squires – Squire Western, for example – is a town joke; people wince away from the mud, the loud sporting laughter, the gross manners. Wenches may abound but they are thought of as nymphs. London is learning manners and conversation from Addison, Steele and the *Spectator* writers, drinking tea or chocolate – at least polite London is. The rest is soaked in gin, drunk for a penny, dead drunk for twopence. There are always two sides to the London coin. Building is good. The formality of the squares is not superb, but it is satisfying and indicates a belief in proportion and balance. The age was certain – or, rather, certainty existed between 1740 and 1780. In this time lived a generation of men, says Trevelyan, 'wholly characteristic of the 18th century ethos, a society with a mental outlook of its own, self-poised, self-judged and self-approved, freed from the disturbing passions of the past and not yet troubled with anxieties about a very different future'.

One can say that the sense of a future was mostly a spiritual luxury or fright peculiar to the nineteenth century. Until then Londoners lived bluffly and sensibly without it. They were able to do so because they had constructed for themselves a world of classical certainties and orthodoxy: every utterance of Dr Johnson conveys this. 'It was an age,' says Trevelyan, 'of aristocracy and liberty, of the rule of law and the absence of reform, of individual liberty and institutional decay; of Latitudinarianism above and Wesleyanism below; of the growth of humanitarian and philanthropic feeling and endeavour; of creative vigour in all the arts and trades that serve to adorn the life of man.'

The London squares were not built by a Napoleonic planner, but by private enterprise: by aristocratic and financial speculators. The rule of law was severe; in a hundred years the victory of Parliament eventually created a gentry who put their money into wool and cotton. Their passion for property and for defending it increased the number of hanging crimes from fifty to two hundred. The mass of the population were decimated by drinking raw gin. When the Government at last stopped this by slapping on a huge tax, the terrible death rate declined, though some of the credit must go to the humane impulses Trevelyan mentions. But Londoners were far better fed than they were to be in the nineteenth century; the great hospitals – Guy's, Westminster, and Middlesex – were built; medicine improved. And when one looks at exemplary heroes held up as models to the readers of the novels of Goldsmith, Fielding and Sterne, they are quixotic men of simple humanity. Goodness, it will be noted, in a worldly age, is thought to be an eccentric and blessed innocence. Against the savage, criminal mind of Jonathan Wild we see the simple, gullible citizen Heartfree. The improvement of public morals is a command to which almost all subscribe. All know – for so set and certain was the trite, hard eighteenth-century mind – what Virtue is and what is Vice: no one more than Richardson in *Pamela* and *Clarissa*, whose two heroines convey the ambiguous domestic ideal of the time. One reads, at first with astonishment, Trevelyan's statement 'that the proportion of men of genius per head of population in the irregularly educated England of George III was immensely greater than in our day'; and then one recalls that the population of England was only five and a half millions in the reign of Queen Anne, rising to nine in the Napoleonic wars, and that London in Dr Johnson's time had only 600,000 people. That appears to be the ideal size for a capital city if it is to be surpassing in amenity and brains.

A civilisation had attained excellence and equanimity; its conflicts had passed the point of destructiveness and intolerance, had fused and enriched. England had always been the country of craftsmen, and in this century, in the making of china, glassware, silver plate, furniture, they equalled and even surpassed the best work in Europe. If we look from London across the Channel to Paris and compare the conditions under which gifted men and women lived in the two cities, there is one important difference which can be said permanently and profoundly to set off London from the Continent. In Paris a man must go to Court to succeed; the aristocracy have left their estates for Versailles and regard it as shame and defeat if they are banished from that brilliant centre. In England this was not so. London had a dozen Courts, in the houses of the aristocracy, and the Londoner got little prestige, after Elizabethan times, from closeness to the Monarch, although a Wren or a Defoe had much by the way of patronage.

If an impenetrable self-satisfaction seems to have settled on the faces of the middling men and women of the eighteenth century as we see them in the portraits of Reynolds and Gainsborough and Hogarth, a rosy, fleshy and sober determination to be themselves, immovably, we can perhaps trace it to that final implantation of solidarity to class which has distinguished the English since. Individual they may be, eccentricity they will insist on – it is the only escape – but they respond first to what their class, and hence their view of society, demands. They will stick to their conventions, tolerating a great deal in the matter of waywardness or excess, for they know that to conform to what is fitting and civil is a strain. Civility is their ideal, and they furtively recognise that it has a price. Throughout the novels of the eighteenth century we see how much stronger is the idea of man in society than the idea of man on his own. Even when Richardson created that brilliant embodiment of Satanic man in Lovelace, the English Don Juan, we are mainly conscious of him not as pure evil but as a social type of the century's abductor of heiresses at war with the family money system in England, a system that paid lip service to romantic love but which was deeply concerned with the respectable, social, conventional demands of property and the marriage market. And, in this, Lovelace has the glow of the accepted rebel.

And was the eighteenth century so settled, so certain, and so beneficent? We turn to the London of Hogarth – and we see the disorder under the self-possession. Hogarth is an improver. (That is typical of the London that muddles, fails to plan, but is ceaselessly 'improving' and 'repairing', resisting as hard as it can the temptation to get the thing formulated in advance.) He believes in Vice and Virtue. He teaches a moral lesson. Yet he does for London in picture, in camera work, what Defoe reports in print. Many foreigners, even today, express the suspicion, not to say the certainty, that under London good nature, patience and civility, there exists something hard, ruthless, self-mutilating, and, ultimately, brutal. But all civilisations depend on inhibition. In Hogarth's paint and drawing, one sees a terrifying London. It is the London he saw when he wandered into the Covent Garden of his time, the centre of the brothels, the crime, the rough pleasures of the city. The place is hearty, roaring and violent in the gin-drinking days. Hogarth's black-and-white sense of evil owes something to Puritan insensibility, and critics of *The Rake's Progress* in his own time pointed out that few rakes came to a bad end, and that the attraction of pleasure is its pleasurableness. But the famous harlots and procurers did exist; they went sometimes to the gallows, and what strikes one about Hogarth is the minuteness of his observation. Like Pepys, like Defoe, he is intensely interested in every detail of the external world, in every detail of the dress and habits of innumerable Londoners.

They lived, it is clear, far more in the street than we do, and, as always in London, the place names survive. The Adam and Eve public house in Tottenham Court Road, where he took his stand for his picture *The March to Finchley*, still exists – though it is not the original. *Marriage à la Mode* is not only a diverting and terrible story of London society, but it is exactly one of the time, for it represents the marriage of a rich tradesman's daughter and the heir to an earldom. The unfinished Palladian house of the earl – he got his architecture from Italy, as became an aristocrat –

can be seen through the window of the room where the betrothal takes place: and in the morning-after scene, when the marriage is breaking up, one sees the still vigorous, sly, seductive young wife, full of spirit, while her husband, exhausted by a night out in Covent Garden, sprawls dead white in a chair, and with a woman's cap stuck in his pocket. In the following *Visit to the Doctor*, we see the consequences of the night out: the young nobleman is being offered pills to cure – it has been conjectured – syphilis. Hogarth sought out real faces: Moll Hackabout of *The Harlot's Progress* was recognised by everyone as old Mother Needham, the bawd whose house was near St James's Palace and who, after being exposed twice on the pillory, where she was pelted by the crowd, died in prison.

There is a firm refusal of the idealising imagination in Hogarth's work. His kind of imagination composes. It fills in the bold outline of life with fidelity to its due, sensuous content. His people have the subdued hum of mundane living in their ears. His is an art that conveys whatever may be passing idly through the heads of his sitters in that lethargic hour. At first sight he is prosaic; then we notice the subtlety of texture, the minute sensuous brilliance of selected detail. He respects his subjects. Ordinary or uncouth, his women breathe. He draws the person. He has the Londoner's ruminative satisfaction in character and in the comedies of self-respect. His people are passable company, and he catches them – this is his special gift – on the point of change from one mood to another, in action. The Staymaker is about to turn round; Mrs Salter will make one of her dull but determined remarks. The feeling is the prosaic one out of which comedy is born. His contribution to English painting was urban: the conversation piece that does not sit still, but is something staged like a scene from a film that has been stopped for a moment but will, in a second or two, become animated. The amount of real and expected movement in Hogarth is remarkable and, when the latter comes, it will be as rude, pushing and energetic and petulant as he himself was. The well-known account of his trip to Ramsgate is a rough affair, of drinking, scuffling, fighting, practical joking and horse-play; it reminds us that behind the rational surface his part of the eighteenth century presented, there was violence. And that the assumption of rationality was an assertion of the mind's capacity to impose order on a world that was dramatic and disorderly. The more composed, trite or elegant the voice, the more violent the fight in the street outside. Walpole said that to travel across London at certain hours was to take one's life in one's hands; he was attacked by highwaymen returning from Holland House: coaches were held up in Piccadilly, so thronged it was by rogues. Dryden was beaten up by the servants of the Earl of Rochester in Covent Garden. And Fielding, gentleman, playwright and novelist, was the hard-drinking magistrate who took on the job of clearing up the crime of the London streets. The aristocracy despised him for it, especially when they found him dining with his housekeeper and, at the same time, dealing with a gang of ruffians who had been brought to his house by the Watch.

The realism of the eighteenth century is seen, in another way, in Swift, the realism of the magnifying glass – Pepys's magnifying glass that the highwayman stole from him and failed to return as he had promised. The realism is as coarse as it is in Hogarth, but in Swift's case edged by fantasy, and fear of – what? Time, madness. Richardson, too, stares long at all the detail of life. Think of his account of the bawd's hair standing up like hog's bristles! Think of the precision of Dryden's prose, the prose of a clear, fierce, satirical mind. Johnson's mind is like clear plain glass; he is certain every time he utters, and if he has to record a change of opinion, he does so with that additional certainty, that additional sense of experience that pugnacity or irony give. He knocks down matters that require knocking down, with a bang, like a man pitching a heavy ball at skittles. The ball booms, the skittles scatter with a bang which is half laughter.

Why are these men of genius so certain? Why was their London so sure? The merchant and citizen were in their element; the world was limited; where passion was obviously uncontrolled, before their very eyes, they dealt with it blandly by calling it Folly or Vice and that was that. Doubt

125

was not to arise until sensibility and sentiment came in. Johnson dismisses Rousseau – as a conservative will dismiss anything novel – as an intelligent man playing for effect and making fools of his audience; just as people used to say the Post-Impressionist painters were clever cynics pulling our legs and laughing up their sleeves at us.

In the first part of the eighteenth century, London rejoiced in the certain knowledge that it was new born in its red brick; in the second half, it began to wonder why it was born and for what. If Johnson is all certainty, Boswell is all experiment, speculation, introspection, doubt, wonder at himself. In the very act of intercourse with a cheap harlot in the street, on Westminster Bridge, he wonders at his nerve, the price, the mystery of his lusts and his 'genius'; Sterne sees his very consciousness in a state of dissolution. The proper study of mankind is man, but man melts away before one's eyes. He is dirty, sensual, climbing, vain, idealistic, feeling, crying, pushing, sensitive, mad, brilliant. They excel, all these writers and talkers, as conscious or unconscious auto-biographers. Life is made for conversation. And that is what they conceived London to be; a place where one could talk well. When Boswell said the place was too large and that he thought of retiring to a desert, Johnson told him he had desert enough in Scotland. 'The happiness of London,' Johnson said, 'is not to be conceived but by those who have been in it. I will venture to say there is more learning and science within the circumference of 10 miles from where we now sit, than in all the rest of the Kingdom.'

Johnson loved the city for its talk. It took place in clubs, especially in The Club which met in Soho. The members talked freely and, often (since London was split by violent party and personal differences), with a satirical vindictiveness which has never been heard since. The more 'set' a society is, the more savage the satire. By the nineteenth century clubs had become conformist and respectable; it was not done to talk politics or religion freely, and the smooth arts of gentlemanly evasion and persiflage were invented. Certain subjects were excluded, just as certain people were excluded from the conversation of the new upper middle class and the rich business men who governed social life. The gentleman was not speechless; but he was committed to conversational formulae.

But the eighteenth century lay down a manner of talk that has never quite died. There have always been pockets of it, and it was, in fact, considerably revived in the twenties in Bloomsbury and the Universities. Good London talk – if we can risk a definition – is, before anything else, light, sociable, discursive, enquiring, personal without vulgar reserves, prone to fantasy, never too serious, avoids entering the wilderness of the merely informative, the expert and the didactic – a bore is the man who tells you everything – does not lay down the law except as a matter of personal idiosyncrasy, and is regarded as a relaxation and not as a means to an end. It sedulously avoids the professional, never harangues and is enhanced – or ruined, according to your view – by the amateur spirit. London talk has a horror of conclusions, and some foreigners have been exasperated by its fundamental eccentricity, though they have been charmed by its skilful evasions. Henry Adams despised it. And if foreigners turn to very ordinary society – the local meeting of mixed people who may be shopkeepers, factory workers, clerks, any collection who have got together out of the mass – they often express their astonishment at the articulateness of these people when they talk about their own experience, the fluency with which they utter opinion, their free display of individual character, their surly power of debate, a firm and inborn knowledge of how to discuss the matter in hand. If a Londoner is without conversation, it is because he has decided, at that moment, that he 'owes it to himself' to be without it.

If from the time of Pepys onwards the recognisable Londoners appear and establish a type, visible London also puts on an appearance in brick and stucco that was to be its habit well into the nineteenth century, and that still gives the centre of the city its style. I think of the long sparrow-brown streets of three- or four-storey houses, with their arched or porticoed doorways, their fan-lights, their long windows – which have made architects describe the city as 'vertical' even though it has little height – their basements, and their railings. Rows of doorways, rows of windows, each house like a mild and spectacled face. Brick has triumphed domestically, as at Hampton Court it has triumphed regally. Brick, ruddy or blackened, houses the Inns of Court – the Temple, Lincoln's Inn and Gray's Inn – and gratefully sets off the green of the plane trees, their sweeping and romantic boughs and their lawns. This London has often been denounced as a monotonous collection of little boxes; it seemed 'soulless' to some Victorians. For myself, the London of the little houses, whether they are in Harley Street or Chelsea, Islington or Kensington, and the millions of little chimneys, is the true London. Gower Street is being pulled down now to house new portions of London University, in the new stone architecture suitable to, say, Dartmoor Prison or Holloway; but enough of this street, so often condemned as featureless, still remains to convey the subtle colouring of London brick. The browns, blacks, reds and ochres, the varieties of grey, in a London brick wall change with the weather, the light, the time of day, and are as tender as plumage. London's genius for the excluding wall has had a confederate in the weather; and what to the impatient or dramatic eye appears to be blank and without distinction is to the active and curious eye rich in texture, sensuous and warm. The absence of show, the worn decency of these streets, enhances their individuality so that, in each of the houses, sordid or well kept, one notices a meditative air and one knows that, in each, the meditation and business of the day is different. From the oldest of these streets to the later ones, one is aware of the mysterious changes of social standing, of the survival of some hierarchies and the passing of others. The fact is that one is passing not only from one close of self-complacency to another, but from age to age and, far stronger than either of these, from village to village.

After the Fire, London moved out into squares. Lincoln's Inn Fields, where Nell Gwynn was born, were a pleasure ground and haunt of thieves, but the lawyers had fine houses from 1720 onwards; before this, Bloomsbury Square and St James's Square established themselves for wealth and fashion. The squares of London exist because they stood on land owned by the nobility who turned to speculative building. As the estates were entailed, squares have remained, even when they have been ruined, as Soho Square, Berkeley Square, Grosvenor Square, Hanover Square have been; indeed it is difficult to think of more than three or four good ones left. Sometimes the nobleman built, sometimes a craftsman, a bricklayer, a capitalist, even an actor. The squares gave London the one quality that has made life tolerable – at least in the centre – in a place of the size. For the square was designed to be a little village in itself, with a green and trees in the middle, its shopping streets, its less expensive streets for servants, employees, and so on nearby.

The speculators – this was notoriously so in the case of Hanover Square, built in 1717 – made one misjudgement. They built in the expectation that one or two of the central houses would be mansions of the aristocracy, but this ambition failed except in the case of St James's: the aristocracy put all their money into their country houses. It was the City men who moved in. This is vividly recorded in Thackeray's *Vanity Fair*, where by the time of the Napoleonic wars, the new-rich Osbornes, who made money out of the inflation, moved west into Russell Square. And when one has in mind the host of figures, memorable in English history and scandal, notable in life, famous in government, literature, sciences and the arts, it is this London, of this very brick, that housed them all and appointed their daily life. Their world is within the reach of the most casual perambulator of the London streets.

4

By the beginning of the nineteenth century, the population of London had risen to 1,274,000; that is to say, in a hundred years it had doubled and the smoke of the sea-coal blackened its skies. The Industrial Revolution had begun, and, with it, before very long, a change in the mood of Londoners became plain.

In the eighteenth century, London was optimistic about itself and pessimistic about the rest of the world. It lived comfortably in the aura of its patriotic songs – the best in the English genre belong to this period – trusting in its 'hearts of oak', 'eating the roast beef of old England'; in all classes, at the beginning of that century, people ate well. The optimism did not connote a belief in Progress; but, rather, a belief in equanimity. The world had, thank heaven, stopped still. With the Industrial Revolution and the founding of the second British Empire after the liberation of America and the war with France, the intoxicating belief in energy, expansion and Progress set in, with London in the lead. The face of the city was turned away from the Continent; since then, generation by generation, the British separation from the Continent and the assertion of Britain's fundamental difference from Europe have increased until the present day. For a century, at any rate, that assertion triumphed to an extent so great that it can be said to have assured the peace of the world.

Externally, the Pax Britannica, a hundred years of peace; internally, what? And how did the London idea differ from the continental? The capital was not the despotic centre of a military system, nor of illiberal politics. Its aristocracy differed, say, from the French, in that the English aristocracy were not cut off from public life first by Court and then by revolution. Its masses, even when victimised, did get some local relief – it is true, of a hard-faced kind. Its middle class was vastly more numerous and secure than were those in Europe, and the wealth of the Industrial Revolution slowly but effectively softened those differences between men of talent or energy and 'men of rank' that made the Continent draw blood. But the onset of the Industrial Revolution was savage. The workless craftsmen and small traders came hungrily, in hundreds of thousands, into the cities, and for generations industrialism made the rich richer and the poor poorer. It was a tragedy that Britain received the shock of the greatest transformation which human life had received for perhaps two thousand years – and was the first country in the world to feel it – in the midst of the Napoleonic wars and a fight for existence. Those wars had wrecked the national economy; industrialism and the second Empire were to save it, but without the guidance of precedent or preparation and at an appalling price.

London did not suffer the degree of self-destruction which occurred in the manufacturing North. It was a commercial city. It did not live by the machinery of iron ore, wool and cotton. It sold and shipped the product. The masses swarmed in from the ruined rural life. The slums appeared, and out of the slums poured the London mob, breaking the windows of the clubs, taunting the Duke of Wellington, while government spies hunted out the members of Jacobin societies. Cobbett tells the tale for rural England. Disraeli, looking back, described 'the two Englands' that lived side by side: the hellish cities of the hungry, where the children earned more than their parents, and the kind of life that went extravagantly on in the country house and the town mansion. Trevelyan says:

In the past, poverty had been an individual misfortune; now it was a group grievance. It was a challenge to the humanitarian spirit which the Eighteenth Century had engendered. That spirit had been obscured for awhile by England's angry fright at the French Revolution, but in the new Century it could no longer regard the victims of economic circumstance with the hard indifferent eye of earlier ages.

But what must have amazed the foreign visitor to London between, say, 1790 and 1830 was the elegance, the splash and the grandeur of the new London. If old Sedley had been ruined, the Osbornes had moved in to Vanity Fair. The lights might be out in Europe, but they glittered in London; and when the war was over and the poor rioted, they blazed.

One manifestation which had more than a passing influence was Byronism. All Europe, even Russia, adopted it. Another was dandyism in the genius of Beau Brummell. Beau Brummell is often presented to us as a man who spent his morning tying a neckcloth, and therefore the epitome of extravagant folly. He was not. Puritanically, he brought good sense and simplicity into dress and manners. He also introduced the notion that personal cleanliness was important. It can be said of Brummell that he set the tone for those who stayed at home during the Napoleonic wars, and, of course, most people did stay at home. Born in 1778, he was the son of a man who became private secretary to Lord North, went to Eton, and inherited a large fortune. But he was the grandson of a man who let lodgings to the nobility in St James's, and, reverting perhaps to a good servant's sense of what is proper, became an arbiter of dress and manners to his betters. He was, after he had met the Regent, the Jeeves of his period, who abhorred ostentation. He stood quite alone, determined to be undefeatable by royalty, aristocracy and anyone else, on their own ground. He instituted the notion, at least in dress, that the duty of a gentleman was to be inconspicuous. After the Napoleonic wars, the English became the fashion in France; dandyism was absorbed by them into the Romantic movement: one became a London dandy, bored, impassive, androgynous, insolent and keen on horses. It was known as dressing à la Valtre-Scott! Dandyism became, of course, conceptualised in France (Miss Ellen Moers's *The Dandy* is worth reading on the subject) and was in fact an anti-bourgeois movement. In England it started as a Puritan protest – for that is what Brummell's campaign was, London manners always being in need of improvement or, at any rate, of being pointed up like London brick. The important difference between the dandyism of London and of Paris is that London took the lesson and regarded the rest as unuseful, superficial and foolish; whereas the French saw it as a revolutionary gesture.

Beside Beau Brummell we must put John Nash, the Regent's architect, the author of the last large enterprise of planning that London was to know. It is the final expression of a classical age, exhibitionist, decadent, no doubt, but superb, a last stand before the Victorian grotesque swept the city. Crabb Robinson, the diarist and talker, the famous giver of breakfast parties, the friend of Lamb, Coleridge and Wordsworth, wrote of Nash's Carlton House in the Mall:

> I really think this enclosure with the new street leading to it from Carlton House, will give a sort of glory to the Regent's government which will be more felt by remote posterity than the victories of Trafalgar and Waterloo, glorious as these are.

Remote posterity does indeed feel gratitude. I take the quotation from Sir John Summerson's eloquent book on Nash. The architect, he says, was a lesser artist than Brummell: one brought in starched shirts, the other the stucco facade, but 'never attained the quintessential and absolute mastery of style that Brummell achieved in dress'. The comparison is apt, for whatever may be said of Nash's work, he unquestionably dressed the city. At the corner of Bloomsbury Square near the British Museum one can see his house and see the fanciful stucco facings he put on the plain London brick that bored him. He wanted London to vie with Paris.

Nash grew up on the wharves of Lambeth and the decaying pleasure grounds. He was a bounder, a humorist, a wit, immensely knowledgeable. He loved large undertakings and large financial speculations. An estate – Marylebone Park – had reverted to the Crown. There were two possible plans. One, to cover the huge area from St James's Park northwards as far as the new Regent's Canal running through north London with another set of Bloomsbury squares; the other – Nash's plan – was to create a huge garden city for the aristocracy, with parks, groves and pleasant panoramas. Nash was lucky in an intimate acquaintance with the Prince of Wales: it has been said that Nash obliged the Prince by marrying the Prince's mistress. The ambition of the architect was to outdo the Paris of Napoleon. The grandiose scheme was never realised to the full, but what was achieved is startling in its grace and its spaciousness. Sir John Summerson writes of the terraces of Regent's Park that they

are dream palaces, full of grandiose, romantic ideas such as an architect might scribble in a holiday sketch book. Seen at a distance, framed in green tracery, perhaps in the kind light of late autumn, they suggest architectural glories which make Greenwich tame and Hampton Court provincial. Carved pediments, rich in allegory, top the trees; massive pavilions, standing forward like the *corps de garde* of Baroque chateaux are linked to the main structures by triumphal arches or columnar screens; each terrace stretches its length in all the pride of unconfined symmetry. It is magnificent. And behind it all – behind it are rows and rows of identical houses, identical in their narrowness, their thin pretentiousness, their poverty of design. Where the eye apprehends a mansion of great distinction, supported by lesser mansions and service quarters, the mind must interpret it as a block of thin houses, with other blocks of thin houses carrying less ornament or none at all. The sham is flagrant and absurd. The terraces are architectural jokes; and though Nash was serious enough in his intention, the effect is an odd combination of fantasy and bathos which only the retrospect of a century can forgive.

Yet where else in this ugly city is there a region with an equal amenity and where the eye is almost continuously pleased and stimulated? There are finer, stranger things, but they are isolated or merge in the heavy London *minestrone*.

Against the picture of wealth, taste and sensibility supreme, we must put the casualties. There is William Blake, who lived through the Industrial Revolution from its beginnings in the eighteenth century and saw his craft, the engraver's, decay, and himself died poor in Lambeth.

And in their stead intricate wheels invented,
Wheel without wheel,
To perplex youth in their outgoings & to bind to labours
Of day & night the myriads of Eternity, that they
                                        might file

139

And polish brass & iron hour after hour, laborious
                                        workmanship,
Kept ignorant of the use that they might spend the
                                        days of wisdom
In sorrowful drudgery to obtain a scanty pittance
                                        of bread,
In ignorance to view a small portion & think that All,
And call it demonstration, blind to all the simple
                                        rules of life.

In 1821 Stendhal came to London and went with some timid
friends, armed to the teeth, to visit what they had been led to
believe was a dangerous brothel. It was a poor little house,
inhabited by three ill-fed, modest girls, and what astonished
him, after Paris, was their decent misery, their ignorance of
what good food was – never having even heard of it – and
the absence of all natural gaiety. They were not hardened,
they were well-behaved in it, shy, prim, simple-minded and
disheartened. If there was a raucous side to drunken London
poverty, the side Boswell had seen among the jolly prostitutes
of the taverns of the Strand, there was now, fifty years later,
pathos and something grey and mean.

What London was like for half the century is perfectly
established by Dickens, not in documentary realism, as is
sometimes suggested, but as an extraordinary brew of hard
fact and imagination. It contains not only the place and

people in their huge variety, but also what they felt themselves and it to be. It has often been pointed out that Dickens was not a political thinker, and that he did not know the Industrial Revolution and the life of the poor by their kind of experience, but by the eye and ear of the southern, genteel and commercial lower middle class, despite what he may have seen in the blacking factory or in the Marshalsea prison. It has been shown that he is an unreliable historian, for he commonly married events from his childhood with those of later years; that the romance of the old coaching days was well over in Mr Pickwick's time; that he frequently attacked the philanthropists who were working for reform; and that when he back-dated and made fun of the Circumlocution Office, he was mocking one of the major Victorian achievements: the foundation of an honest and able permanent civil service. (He was right in showing it to be a sort of family patrimony.) Like most Englishmen he was extremely class-conscious. But only a fool goes to Dickens for hard facts. He was not a Gradgrind. He is the Victorian age, his portion of it, in person. It was a violent and histrionic time. Dickens was a dandy and an actor; his waistcoats were as gorgeous as Disraeli's; he vastly admired Brummell's successor, the Count d'Orsay. He was theatrical in remorse, familiar with melodrama in real life. The great animal energies of Victorian Londoners were diverted by moral pressure to concentration on work, the pursuit of money and the power the machine had given them. The worship of work was itself a violence. The suppression of the bedroom in the novel did not mean that the bedroom did not exist; the stress on the domestic virtues only too plainly shows that they were precarious. Victorian respectability was not a placid shield, but the aggressive weapon of ambition, the defence if failure assailed; the famous masochism was a means of rising in the world.

Dickens both sees these things and does not see them, because he *is* them, in person. A climber, he can accurately describe the successful Veneerings; mutilated by success, he can describe what the Dombeys have done to themselves. It used to be said that Dickens was a caricaturist who took one or two dominant traits in a man or woman and exaggerated them; and it is certainly true that in the *Sketches by Boz* this is how he began. But, in fact, the London mind runs easily to fantasy and self-caricature and most certainly did so in Dickens's time. The solemn, preoccupied business men walking in the street, whom Stendhal saw, were quite other inside their heads. They were conscious of living in a personal drama and of acting a private role, and this, as an actor, Dickens perceived. All the comic characters of Dickens inflate themselves; all the straight characters head for some moral climax which will be melodramatic. Even Little Nell and Little Dorrit are self-inflated, pretending to a private style. 'Me and mother is very 'umble' is Uriah

Heep's inner theme song, his bid for rank, place and role. By it he stakes a claim to be something, if only a worm, in the society he lives in, as certainly as Pecksniff, Pip and Micawber do. This quality of consequence is certainly a London quality, but it has another aspect. It is the sign of an inner life and of an inner dialogue, the habit of soliloquy, romantic, sentimental, fanciful, eccentric, childish, nonsensical, ribald, comic, imaginative, hypocritical, self-mocking. It is a personal, reflective poetry, the projection of reminiscence or of dream, a sign that they live doggedly, tenaciously, fatalistically alone, sustained by their strange histories.

> ... if you ever contemplate the silent tomb, sir, which you will excuse me for entertaining some doubt of your doing, after the conduct into which you have allowed yourself to be betrayed this day; if you ever contemplate the silent tomb, sir, think of me. If you would wish to have anything inscribed upon your silent tomb, sir, let it be, that I – ah my remorseful sir! that I – the humble individual who has now the honour of reproaching you, forgave you.

That is Pecksniff, but it might be the hall porter of a London hotel who has just done you down; the absconding cashier; the man who stopped me in Holborn yesterday and told me the police were watching him and 'I ain't done nothing'. It is also Eliot's Londoner gravely crossing London Bridge, and greeting another Stetson. There are – we are assured – no

143

more midwives like Sairey Gamp, though I have seen many old nurses hanging about the all-night chemists nowadays whose style and fancies are similar to hers; but her soliloquies are notable for a range of imagination which is commonly met and which show how closely Londoners fuse with their environment. It is as if they grew out of the damp pavements or the floors of the public bars like plants, their special fancy being funereal.

'Which, Mr Chuzzlewit,' she said, 'is well-beknown to Mrs Harris as has one sweet infant (though she *do* not wish it known) in her own family by the mother's side, kep in spirits in a bottle; and that sweet babe she see at Greenwich Fair, a travelling in company with the pink-eyed lady, Prooshan dwarf, and livin' skelinton, which judge her feelings when the barrel organ played, and she was showed her own dear sister's child, the same not being expected from the outside picter, where it was painted quite contrairy in a livin' state, a many sizes larger, and performing beautiful upon the Arp, which never did that dear child know or do; since breathe it never did, to speak on, in this wale!'

The passage is a London poem; its subject the Victorian death rate.

Dickens's London is Gothic, in fancy and in terror; his imagination owes something to the hurt done to a mind formed by the eighteenth century and injured by the nineteenth; he is true to an aspect of London's inner life, and there is much that is permanent to the city in him. So much do Dickens 'characters' still abound that writers are sometimes reproached for prolonging a cliché if they still put them down.

The Victorians' attitude to the past is marked by anomalies and peculiar accidental influences. There is the long influence of the Romantic movement and particularly the influence of Scott, who issued the romantic Highland past to the whole of Europe at the beginning of the century and yet, in his contemporary scenes, wrote in the spirit of the middle-class domestic ideal. Scott's feeling for pageantry and romance coloured the Victorian mind. Bulwer-Lytton in *Pelham* provided Europe with the figure of a dandy less local than Beau Brummell. His *Pelham* inspired Carlyle's denunciation in *Sartor Resartus*. Carlyle's philosophy of clothes was exotically dressed up in a prose that is a real Victorian mixture of Biblical, German and Gaelic substance, a prose thoroughly gargoyled. One sees so many elements in the Victorian outlook: industrialism was destroying the picturesque; *vive* the picturesque. Only one basic dislike puts unity in the general disorder: the dislike of the rational 'immoral' eighteenth century and of the classical ideal. It is felt to be heartless, licentious, tedious, affected, dull. Ruskin cries, in *Modern Painters*: 'Now listen to the cold-hearted

Pope say to a shepherd girl, "Where'er you walk cool gales shall fan the glade.'" It is, he says, 'simple falsehood, uttered by hypocrisy'. Only Thackeray, the child of nabobs, the Anglo-Indian, a foreigner to the English scene by family upbringing, has a long sentimental indulgence for the period in *Henry Esmond*. George Eliot goes to the Renaissance for *Romola*; Tennyson revives the Knights of the Round Table; in William Morris, the social revolt and vision is put into the head of the leader of the English peasant rising of 1381, John Ball. If the new manufacturers saw themselves in strange medieval costume, so – with real justification – did Morris see socialism. And it was not only the English past that was reconquered and colonised by the Victorian imagination; but the past of other cultures. True that, in its own time, the eighteenth century had seen itself dressed in the mind of classical antiquity, but this was in the formal and static manner that suited their composed attitude to life. The Victorians were for the active, the energetic and expansive. The discovery of Persian poetry, from Ferdowsi to Saadi, is an instructive case: it was the work of Anglo-Indian officials, the servants of Empire, who translated an immense quantity of Persian verse into English while they governed. Matthew Arnold writes *Sohrab and Rustum*; Browning plants himself in the Italian past; in painting, the Pre-Raphaelite movement establishes its colonies in legend. The impulse was not, indeed, purely English: it was felt by all the Romantics. But in England these subjects were pursued with an earnest, personal and almost proselytising Protestant zeal. And if one looks into the mind of the ordinary Londoner going to his Nonconformist chapel, now at the height of its success and wholly representative of the thriving industrious middle class, it was coloured by the vivid and exotic imagery of the Bible, an imagery which it applied to such splendid exotic opportunities as the rise of Garibaldi. The London mind was always abroad somewhere, in past and present. It was perhaps a rich and indigestible Christmas pudding; and indeed the overeating that went on in family life in the thriving classes is mentioned metaphysically by Meredith, who, not noticing that the vice had spread to his own style, pronounced in *Beauchamp's Career* that, by the seventies, England was stiff with surfeit and on the point of apoplexy.

It is the era not only of the medieval revival in the arts, but in architecture; when the clear light of the churches was being historicised and beglamoured with the new stained glass. Few men stood out against this self-congratulating alliance with history. Clough – not a success as a poet in his generation – had the nerve to write:

Rome disappoints me much; I hardly as yet
                              understand, but
Rubbishy seems the word that most exactly
                              would suit it . . .

147

and

> Ye gods! what do I want with this rubbish of
> ages departed,
> Things that nature abhors, the experiments she
> has failed in?

For the rest, history gave clothes and emotions for the citizens to dress up in as they sat in the counting-houses of Cornhill, or lived on Disraeli's 'sweet simplicity of the three per cents'.

In architecture the most powerful manifestation of the historic spirit and one that detaches London most clearly from the cities of the Continent is the Gothic revival. It was meant to do so. In that great age London felt the long deference to the Continent was almost immoral and that in turning to Gothic it was returning to its own honest traditions and nature. London had been Gothic before the Fire; let it recover its native past. And it is true that the chapel of Henry VII at Westminster is one of London's glories.

So many influences, so many persuasive hints from the past hang over the rebirth of this ancient style at the height of London's modernity and leadership in the world. In the first place, the use of the arts and crafts movements as an aesthetic protest against the machine found substance in the fact that Gothic had never quite ceased to be the typical way of building in the countryside. The splendid old barns of the

English farms are essentially Gothic constructions, carried on by builders' habit from century to century; and in the country towns stand the Gothic cathedrals. Another influence was literary – the revival of interest in Milton and Spenser and the onset of the German aspects of the Romantic movement. No man could have been more of a Germanophile than Carlyle, who somehow made the Germanic sound religious, revolutionary, and patriotic to Victorian ears. Finally, there is Ruskin, who found in the Gothic not only the work of craftsmen, but an aspiring idealism and a spirit that resisted the 'enervating sensuousness' of the Renaissance. The opponents of Gothic suggested that the pointed arch was a Roman Catholic trap; the supporters were able to feel that the Gothic was signally Protestant. The Gothic revival indeed abounds in the comedies of controversy, for the term was a broad one that might take its examples from English Perpendicular or Venice; and when the movement had established itself and infected the jerry-builders of the London suburbs, Ruskin wrote in remorse to the *Pall Mall Gazette*:

I have had an indirect influence on nearly every cheap villa builder between this and Bromley; and there is scarcely a public house near the Crystal Palace but sells its gin and bitters under pseudo-Venetian capitals copied from the Church of the Madonna of Health or Miracles

149

of Morades. And one of my powerful notions for leaving my present house is that it is surrounded everywhere by the accursed Frankenstein monster indirectly of my own making.

The Gothic revival was a matter for irony and comic horror by the twenties of this century, as one can see from Sir Kenneth Clark's book on the subject. (He has since, like many of us, recanted now that we are faced by the glass-house architecture of today.) But when he writes that the beginnings of the movement were literary, he says something that is historically true and also of particular signific-ance in the London temper. The English genius in the arts has been, above all, literary; it has fed on the associations of the mind rather than on the delights of the eye; and before the Victorian influences began to play upon taste, Walpole's Gothic novel and the Gothicising of his house at Strawberry Hill, the translation of Percy's *Reliques of Ancient English Poetry*, and the novels of Scott had made their mark. The new Gothic was first of all a nostalgic fancy, an idealisation of the past; then it moved from the romantic to the religious and from that to the assertion of national idiosyncrasy, faith and virtue. Augustus Welby Pugin, the engaging son of a French émigré, was the founder architect, and it was he who inculcated the principle that gave the movement its force for the Victorians: no Christian should reproduce pagan forms. When the new House of Commons was built after 1834, the classical style was not acceptable. The competition for the designs demanded either a Gothic or Elizabethan style, and that mixture Charles Barry and Pugin provided. And so we have those enormous Gothic buildings that still stamp the Victorian character on London: after the House of Commons, there are the Law Courts, the strange pink cathedral of St Pancras Station, the even odder cathedral of the Prudential Assurance Company in Holborn, and a large number of church-like office blocks. Yet in spite of the proliferation of the pillars of Venetian Gothic on banks, pubs, town halls, shops and villas, or the sudden leap back to the thirteenth century at the Law Courts, the Gothicists did not have it all their own way. The Italian Renaissance was drawn upon and the French. By the end of the century we had the Dutch and, in the suburbs, the Tudor. Distinct as these styles are in the important buildings, they become sooty-whiskered hybrids in the mass of lesser ones, so that when we say London looks Victorian we mean that the look is heavily historicised, frantically mixed, and the expression of an ebullient individualism. The variety of styles, the humours of decoration, the fantasy expressed in knobs, spheres, gazebos, balconies, turrets, small domes, strange windows, extraordinary roofs and peculiar chimneys, in any one street is extraordinary and, finally, hilarious. The ironwork in the squares, the street

151

railings, the lamps and the balconies is wonderfully varied and distinguishes London from any other city – though good ironwork died with the Victorians and really was at its best in the seventeen-forties. The iron Gothic of Paddington Station and in some of the markets is the unique Victorian contribution to architecture. For one mad, inspired moment in the Crystal Palace they produced something original, but, alas, the place was burned down – with shattering propriety – at the time of the abdication. Lions and sphinxes, white horses, a whole zoo of stylised animals, not to mention a dumb population of workaday statues built into the walls of shops add something bizarre to the scene, and, particularly, the pathos of our naive belief in nature. I know no city in which the streets are so different from one another, where the ends of streets are so varied in vista; one is not a Londoner until one's eye begins to enjoy this comedy of reckless and hopeful detail. Whatever is said about Victorian London, it has façades and skylines that divert the fancy. The whole place has an air that is incurably anecdotal and original, dreadfully given to the banalities of nostalgia; even its pomposities are naive and announce a modesty of enterprise. In no other city can one so cheerfully enjoy the accidents of bad art.

Novelists and painters flourished; the drama, although there were excellent actors, was dead. It was dead for pretty well a century. It lived only in the rollicking music halls, which were afloat on beer and spirits, for the popular sentimental anal-minded and boozy genius of London was driven underground. Brothels abounded. The Haymarket, until very late in Victorian times, was cheerful and gaudy with unabashed sin. In closing the brothels at last, the Victorians drove the prostitutes onto the wet streets; the enormous number of these women astonished the foreigners who had supposed – from the Victorian novel – that the city would be prim and censorious, when it was still, what it has always been, clumsily licentious.

It is worth looking at what Taine said about the London of this time. He knew England well. Unlike Hawthorne, who saw London in roughly the same period, Taine was not prejudiced by chauvinism or touchiness when he arrived in the sixties. As a Frenchman, he felt secure. He saw that the break with the moderate traditions of the Continent was complete in spite of the strong Germanic influences of our very German Monarchy. London's foreign trade was more than that of France, Germany and Italy put together and three or four times that of the United States. The thing was apparent in the cheerful, not to say brutal and expatiating self-regard of the ordinary citizen. And what did that gentle-man look like? Taine went to the Derby and drew a generic portrait. The Londoner, according to him, was a large, red-faced man with flabby cheeks and dewlaps; there were the full ginger whiskers, unexpressive blue eyes – some

Americans have spoken of the London face as vacant or absent, as one in which expression has been, or can instantly be, drained away – enormous trunk; general colour full-blooded pink; weight of carcase 240 pounds. And Taine goes on to the truculent muzzle and the large, knotted hands that suggested the primal Teuton as he emerged from the forests, if one reduced the volume of blood and fat, but retained the angular and uncouth bone structure! Rude health was the condition.

A day at the Derby soon brought it out and, in any case, damp, raw London and the heavy food suited its inhabitants. They produced male animals like this one, and women who were either as beautiful as goddesses or like sticks of asparagus. The climate drove one indoors: Sunday was a horror and a speciality that London has never been able to change. (The truth about the misery of London Sundays is that for a couple of centuries at least a great part of the population leaves the city for beery junketings and sports in the country. The country wakes up when London closes down.)

Taine noticed only the abysmal emptiness:

A wet Sunday in London: shops closed, streets almost empty; the aspect of a vast, and well-kept graveyard. The few people in this desert of squares and streets, hurrying beneath their umbrellas, look like unquiet ghosts; it is horrible . . . The rain is small, fine, close, pitiless . . . Feet clatter; there is water everywhere, dirty and impregnated with the smell of soot. A thick, yellow fog fills the air, sinks, crawls on the very ground; at thirty paces a house or a steamship look like ink-stains on blotting paper . . .

Architecture was ruined. Somerset House – which we now think rather fine – was a

> . . . massive and ponderous architecture, with every crevice inked in, porticos foul with soot, a simulacrum of a fountain, waterless in the midst of an empty courtyard, puddles of water on the flagstones, long ranks of blind windows; what can they do in such a catacomb? . . . But, most afflicting of all to the eye are the colonnades, peristyles and Greek ornaments, the mouldings and garlands on the houses, all washed with soot . . .

The side streets off Oxford Street were terrifying slums. Drunks were everywhere, down in the gin cellars, lying on the pavements. The only thing to do in the boredom that had been created was to work, take exercise or drink. Against the opulent life of the aristocracy and upper classes, there was the dulled money-grubbing of the middles with their respectability and their clenched jaws. On the one hand, prosaic home life supported a large and depressed servant class; on the other, people given to gluttony, fighting, drink and prostitution. The natural energy of the people could only be controlled by a stern moral code and plenty of sport. Family life was insensitive and affectionate. Men who kept mistresses did so in a domestic way, not from a sense of adventure, not even with a sense of the illicit, nor with any interest in the varieties of love or passion for their own sakes. Rising young men who could not afford the exorbitant demands of the Victorian wife of the upper classes, settled in St John's Wood with a mistress and lived *en famille*. The Frenchman was saddened at seeing sin so tame. A French mother, he said, was the confidante of her son; for a Victorian son to speak with candour to his mother was inconceivable. The members of the father-dominated English family regarded themselves, before anything else, as independent of each other. The old law of primogeniture established the doctrine that the family should *not* hang together. London was deplorably undemocratic, and Taine thought the French family system much better, for just as wealth was better distributed in France, so were the natural affections. French thinking was freer because it was abstract and did not therefore lead to intolerable practical collisions in family life. London – indeed all England – was a place where the institutions were sounder and better than any-where in the world, but where the individual, with his almost morbid individuality, was spiritually impoverished.

One problem that Taine had to settle after all this was

how such a people could have produced a great literature and some of the finest lyrical poetry in the world, not to mention Shakespeare. Since most literature was written in London, and all of it had to submit to London's remorseless judgement, his answer to this question – so often asked by others, especially by the Irish, the Scots and the Welsh – may enlighten us. He thought that we were excellent reporters of our scene but that we had allowed Puritanism to ruin the arts – no painting or music on the high European level. He falls back on an examination of what he calls the ebullient British 'Me', the native egoism which was certainly dominant in the Victorian age and which was brilliantly analysed by Meredith and may be, in fact, a permanent characteristic:

For them, this ego, this mighty Me, is the principal personage of the world. Invisible and all visible things are rallied to him, subordinate to him and their only merit is in becoming aware of him, in corresponding to something in him . . . To have taken so dominant a part, the spiritual being must be strong and absorbing. And so it is as soon as one observes the principal features of English character: the need for independence, the vehemence and pungency of the passions concentrated but controlled, the harsh though silent grinding of their moral machinery, the vast and tragic spectacle which a soul entire furnishes for its contemplation, the custom of looking into the self, the

seriousness with which they have always considered
human destiny, their moral and religious preoccupations,
in short all signs and faculties and instincts which were
already manifest in the pen of Shakespeare and the hearts
of the Puritans.

We have only, he said, to suffer a 'hypertrophy' of this
'Me', and 'for a soul so constituted and disposed, the proper
medium of expression is poetry'. In other words our
literature occurs when the intolerable pressures split us.

Taine is a methodical observer, but under his positive
detachment was concealed the melancholy aesthete who
thought human beings disgusting. He thought that the
Industrial Revolution would get through its troubles and
that – perhaps as a consequence – there would be no future
for civilisation. He did not notice that the Victorians reacted
against what they detested. It is the age of Dickens, Carlyle,
Ruskin, Morris, of Bradlaugh the Radical, of John Bright
and a host of philanthropists and reformers. Wilberforce had
invented new methods of agitation by tracts, subscriptions,
public meetings, leagues and societies which Trevelyan calls
'the arteries of English life', although Dickens and other
comics made fun of them. Victorian London growled at
night with meetings and was thick with committees. Our
cranks do not give up; indeed they are encouraged. London
has always bred them by the thousand, and though it coarsely

sneers at them in public affairs, it always privately and even piously admires them and sometimes gives in. To be a crank, ridiculed and denounced every day in the press, is to be certain of ultimate fame in London when you are old. Our love of tradition is not altogether conservative; it is also a love of our rebellions and heresies. We have a long, heretical past.

Disraeli spoke of the 'two Englands' – a phrase that has stuck – but London could and can display a far larger number than that. By the end of the century, when the place began to burst out into tens of miles of pink-faced suburb and the modern conurbation began, a lower middle class had emerged and were to become more and more powerful. Their struggle was lacerating. They appear in the novel. First of all, in the novels of Gissing, that passive, self-mutilated man who was married to a prostitute and lived seedily off Tottenham Court Road, the ugliest and most ludicrous street in London, given over to the furniture trade. Its back streets are an overflow from Soho; their population is mostly foreign and consists of waiters, one-room tailors, and the sweated labour of the 'rag trade'. Constable lived there before the area 'went down'. Gissing tells of genteel life just above the level of misery, the life aching for refinement and education. His subject is not the London cheerfulness, but the London apathy, the dragging foot, the half-baked mind. As a novelist, Gissing lacks technical competence; his mind is scholarly; but his London is unique because it is a London outside the conventional view of all the English novelists. It is London as a Russian might have seen it. This is not because Gissing is grey in mind and without humour but because (although he is class conscious and is aware of all the graduations of class that the subtle London mind can think of) he gives class a secondary importance. He despises the Class Game and attempts a psychological penetration. And for a Victorian novelist to refuse to play the Class Game or to devote time to that frantic need the English have for 'placing' people before they can know about them was a flat denial of one of the fundamentals of our comedy.

Wells emerged more cheerfully from the little suburban shop in Bromley, and moved towards the smoky, decaying gentility of Mornington Crescent, where property was 'going down'. Sickert, the only addicted London painter, and one who had deep feeling for London's boredom – the customer in the whore's bedroom can hardly work up the energy to take his boots off – was painting the music halls and back rooms of the hotly Socialist borough of St Pancras. Shaw was there too, Borough Councillor, lecturer and street-corner agitator. *The Diary of a Nobody* brought to life the absurd measliness of Holloway, Mr Pooter being the Little Man in full folly. *Three Men in a Boat* celebrated the important social fact that the poor clerks of London offices were breaking out on the spree every weekend on the river. The unprintable masses were on the move, and London was flaunting, once more, its vulgarity like a dirty skirt and spreading its 'jolly old pals' and 'good sorts' over the countryside. A figure as decorous as Henry James used to go to see the Cockneys in their thousands, sporting on the river from Richmond onwards, and was warmed by the gaudy awfulness of the scene. And what he wrote about polite society at this time was, with little adaptation, equally true of the impolite. To have money, he said, was an advantage, but to lack it was not a disgrace. No one is dropped because he has lost his job, failed in the status race or can't 'keep it up'. There was – and is – no money shame in London. There was and is a good deal of disapproval, in all classes, of new wealth: that satisfies London's innate snobbery.

London, James said at a time when social conventions were popularly thought to be 'sticky',

wants above all to be amused; she keeps her books loosely, doesn't stand on small questions of a chop for a chop, and if there be any chance of people's proving a diversion, doesn't know or remember or care whether they have 'called'. She forgets even if she herself have called. In matters of ceremony she takes and gives a long rope, wasting no time in phrases and circumvallations. It is no doubt incontestable that one result of her inability to stand

161

upon trifles and consider details is that she has been obliged in some ways to lower rather portentously the standard of her manners. She cultivates the abrupt – for even when she asks you to dine a month ahead the invitation goes off like the crack of a pistol – and approaches her ends not exactly *per quatre chemins*.

. . . It is not to be denied that the heart tends to grow hard in her company; but she is a capital antidote to the morbid, and to live with her successfully is an education of the temper, a consecration of one's private philosophy. She gives one a surface for which in a rough world one can never be too thankful. She may take away reputations, but she forms character. She teaches her victims not to 'mind', and the great danger for them is perhaps that they shall learn the lesson too well.

Henry James wrote this in 1888. It is, if one reads it in the light of the case of Oscar Wilde, alarming. One is inclined to add only one emollient sentence: that whoever you are and whatever you have done, you will be revered if you reach old age, for then you will look like a hard old walnut or like some beatified infant of boundless cynicism – the London idea of innocence. You will look so sweet that you will be able to get away with anything.

5

AT WESTMINSTER, THE RIVER CHANGES. The long doctoral
façade of the innumerable, pricking spires and turrets of
the Palace of Westminster; Big Ben's brown, enormous
tower under its imperial pagoda, London's grandfather
clock; close to them the Abbey, higher within than any
other cathedral in England but dwarfed to outside view
because one never gets more than half a sight of it; the
school, tacked on to its cloisters, where Ben Jonson, Wren,
Dryden, Cowper and Gibbon were taught – these are a
climax. Here London rules. At the sight, pride goes like a
gong in the sentimental London heart. This, one realises, is
the place where time itself is British, as British as Boadicea.
Melodious in this deception, Big Ben utters the quarters
and the hours in a grave voice that, at night, spreads over
the city. On the radio the hour at Westminster booms
in the ears of the Orkney Islanders, the Irish and the
Welsh, bringing them thoughts of traffic. In the war,

Lord Haw-Haw called this chime the death knell of an empire – well, that bell tolled also for him.

It dawns on one, too, that this is the place of the voice. If London speaks to Britain or the world, it is from this jumble among the trees where Church, State, City and People have their monumental meeting place. Westminster is the ruling village of the agglomeration of villages. The sight is local. Any awe one may feel is so distributed that one ends by finding the grandeur familiar, fragmentary and sad; the place is so accessible, so trodden by daily usage. Except in winter, the neighbourhood is besieged by tens of thousands of foreigners – West Indians, Indians, Pakistani, Africans, Chinese, not to mention the people of the Continent and the two Americas, so that one is startled to hear the common English accent of some surly delegation slouching into Parliament, with their raincoats on their arms, to see their Member. But all of the Indian, Asiatic, African and North American crowd speak English too – a fact which may seem too trite to mention but which, to a Londoner, is always a surprise. Their English, especially the Asiatics' and Indians', is distinctly upper-class and without our common or garden nuances. It occurs to the Londoner that somehow, some-where, at some time, without being aware of it, he taught them and that he is standing at what is both the shrine and power station of a language of which he is the 'onlie begetter' but which has gone far beyond him and is becoming like the universal Latin of the ancient world. The pride he may feel in this will be so great that, in the end, it becomes the resigned pride of a relegated ancestor. He would hardly venture to add the word 'awe' to it, but, like the profoundly English Mr Sapsea, might go so far as to say he felt 'a species of awe'. As he walks across from the Abbey to the appalling, dough-domed conventicle put up by the rich Nonconformists in Edwardian days, and over to Central Hall, a place always in the news for its smart registry-office weddings, he will recall that near here Caxton, the first man to print a book in English, set up his press and printed Chaucer. Caxton had gone to Bruges when he was a young and acting governor of the Merchant Adventurers in the Low Countries: a merchant who began by translating medieval romance. The English mercantile class has had its private sidelines.

One stands, as I say, under Big Ben, at a culmination. One looks eastward from the bridge where Wordsworth, too, looked back upon the ships, towers, domes, palaces that sparkled in his time, that were blackened under Victoria, and that now are lightened in general aspect by the lard-white office blocks of this century. Between Tower Bridge and Parliament, the Victorians bracketed their Gothic London. Big Ben is only a hundred years old; the Houses of Parliament were rebuilt after 1834 when the old House was burned down on the site – how often London has burned;

only Westminster Hall 'goes back'. It goes back to the very beginning, to William Rufus, the riotous son of the French conqueror. One has to imagine a marsh, Canute building his stronghold, then an abbey rising out of the river mists. One has to imagine Edward the Confessor, the monks refusing to sell the land or allow anyone to build near them. One has to imagine a royal house. Standing on the cold flags among the echoes of Westminster Hall under the immense, springing hammer-beam roof, the largest of its time in Europe, one is looking at the place where Parliament began and Simon de Montfort clanged in to enforce it; where thirty kings have been acclaimed and the law held forth, while in the medieval crowd wandered spivs in jerkins, with a wisp of straw sticking out of their shoes, the notorious 'men of straw' who sold themselves as witnesses. Naked and overbearing are the walls. On the steps the tense heraldic beasts are elegant under their little crowns of stone. They have a royal ferocity. Their very eyes have the regal scream. In the gloom of the place, these savage emblems terrify. The power the Hall evokes – I mean the sense of what power deeply is! Tournaments outside; inside, glory, banquets, trials, death sentences. All London swarmed in. Londoners had the right. Pepys wormed his way into the banquet Charles II gave here and carried off four rabbits and a pullet to eat in a corner. Royal sprees went on until George IV's time, when he served up 17,000 pounds of beef, mutton and veal, and

3,000 fowl, to say nothing of soups, pies, hams, cakes, sweets or the fish and lobster. The feasts are a footnote to the true business of the place: Law and the great State trials. Here the historical imagination stirs. Macaulay sets the stage for the trial of Warren Hastings in 1795, a colossal item in the economics and disingenuities of empire; and, in his Churchillian way, rises to a national occasion, swings out the prose and works himself almost to the point of those tears of pleasure that the affectable Victorians were not ashamed of:

There have been spectacles more dazzling to the eye, more gorgeous with jewellery and cloth of gold, more attractive to grown-up children, than that which was then exhibited at Westminster; but, perhaps, there never was a spectacle so well calculated to strike a highly cultivated, a reflecting, an imaginative mind. All the various kinds of interest which belong to the near and to the distant, to the present and to the past, were collected on one spot, and in one hour. All the talents and all the accomplishments which are developed by liberty and civilisation were now displayed, with every advantage that could be derived both from cooperation and from contrast. Every step in the proceedings carried the mind either backward, through many troubled centuries, to the days when the foundations of our constitution were laid, or far away,

167

over boundless seas and deserts, to dusky nations living under strange stars, worshipping strange gods and writing strange characters from right to left. The High Court of Parliament was to sit, according to forms handed down from the days of the Plantagenets, on an Englishman accused of exercising tyranny over the lord of the holy city of Benares, and over the ladies of the princely house of Oude.

The place was worthy of such a trial. It was the great hall of William Rufus, the hall which had resounded with acclamations at the inauguration of thirty kings, the hall which had witnessed the just sentence of Bacon and the just absolution of Somers, the hall where the eloquence of Strafford had for a moment awed and melted a victorious party inflamed with just resentment, the hall where Charles had confronted the High Court of Justice with the placid courage which has half redeemed his fame.

'The informality with which the area [of Westminster] was treated is indeed astonishing,' says the Dr Nikolaus Pevsner in his indispensable and exhaustive book on the Cities of London and Westminster. In the seventeenth and eighteenth centuries, when the old Parliament stood, only the entrance to Westminster Hall was visible above ground. 'Even the flanking turrets were hidden behind accretions containing, among other things, two pubs.' There were more alehouses and coffee-houses nestling under the walls of other parts of the Palace. The incurable London habit, one has to go on saying, is to let things grow as they will, to drift lazily with the ugly course of nature. A Londoner would never treat a horse, a dog or a garden as he has treated his capital city. It must have required an effort of unaccustomed repentance to get rid of the pubs in the interests of that monstrous enemy of ground-rents: a work of art.

It must be said that London has always tolerated the mad – 'He has a right. Leave him alone' – and, of course, driven the madman madder. The present Houses of Parliament were built by Barry, the man who built the Travellers' Club in Pall Mall, one of the pleasantest buildings in London, and an architect of solid talent. It was he who worked on the great design; the madman was Pugin, the son of a French draughtsman, who covered the place with its immense Gothic detail inside and out down to the very inkstands and coat hangers. Pugin was Gothic mad. He was intoxicated by panelling, tracery and blank tracery, foliage, bays, emblems, oriel figures, turrets and pinnacles. He was a marvellous and fertile artist of the kind who is easily broken by committees; he is said to have sketched in a fanatic uproar of story-telling and shouts of laughter. He was a devout Catholic. His end was to commit suicide at the age of forty, and there were dismal rows after his death, chiefly concerned with his share in the general design. It is characteristic of how the building was grown rather than built that the central flèche and the turrets that give a glitter to the skyline were, as Dr Pevsner tells us, afterthoughts made necessary by the devices of the expert on heating and ventilation, Dr David Boswell Reid, who insisted on vertical ducts. There could have been no more exquisite challenge to Pugin than to turn a ventilator into a turret fit for Camelot.

The Palace of Westminster has always been the butt of the classically minded, and anyone who grew up in the early part of this century has been educated in this derision. From the outside the building does not oppress or bore. Its aspect changes with the hours of the day, so that it has a processional and transient lightness. From the river the long sand-brown façade has restraint and regularity, is serious, yet without heaviness. Then the eye is raised to the roof level, and the spires and turrets seem to break out into a pageant-like trooping of lances and banners, at some fantastic Field of the Cloth of Gold. They glitter. One can imagine the trumpets of heralds; and the flag flying from the great Victoria Tower – now divided into air-conditioned rooms for the storing of Parliamentary documents! – tops it off with a royal flourish. Naval men at Greenwich love to see this flag on the skyline, and mention its great size as something almost holy. The two architects, the staid Englishman and the Anglicised Frenchman, between them have created a work of genius, and they did so at the high point of an aesthetic movement. The whole entirely suits the romantic English temperament. It is proper to the time of Dickens, Carroll and Lear, but without the waywardness and nonsense. The order that has been imposed comes from a certain talent for apparel that gives the Londoner's solemn spirit a dignity and wit. In the evening, when the brown river silvers, the scores of Tudor windows return a serene light, the spires blacken and, suddenly, the towers – especially Big Ben – seem tragic and alone. We reflect that the Palace is becoming a lonelier and lonelier monument in the modern world. London became, after this building was put up, an exporter of parliaments all over the world. Barry and Pugin were more or less copied in Budapest, but with more 'splash', and the Hungarian Parliament of the Danube gives one, for a moment, the illusion that one is standing by the Thames; an illusion – no parliament sits there, no crowds swarm familiarly and affectionately around it. London has imposed parliaments, suggested parliaments; they crop up in Africa and Malaysia, often with some of the bewigged trappings with which we run our own; but their history is not long. It has taken centuries of protest, battle, rebellion, State trials, the stupidities of a civil war, a King's execution and stubborn rows from generation to generation to produce what stands by the Thames.

The Members file in to the chamber of the House of

Commons, take a pinch of snuff if they want it from the coffin-like box in which the doorkeeper sits. They bow to the Chair – yet not to the Chair. There was an altar there in old days, and (probably without knowing it) they are bowing to the altar. Never if we can help it do we forget the past in the present. The present chamber replaces the one destroyed in the war and has that lack of distinction that London has often drifted into; to be distinguished is an accomplishment that has been lost by a generation which pursues the common-place with something amounting to pedantry. The present chamber might be an out-of-date municipal library.

Still the never-never land of the Victorian Gothic imagination survives. One is assaulted by two sensations, the religious and the historical, in the light of which the Victorians conducted the business of the most advanced industrial society of the world for three-quarters of a century. Here the police are at their most melting and considerate, the ushers tall and statesman-like in their black. The House is one of those places where London unmistakably does 'the thing' well and with that briskness which the public institution always brings out in our torpid souls. We are, first of all, inheritors. In this attention to the past, the touch and performance are light and clever. The actors know their parts. The public crowd who wait for the Speaker's Procession which passes every day through the light Central Hall have a homely and ludicrous look in this gay Gothic setting; for the defect of a Gothic background is that it makes twentieth-century man and woman look vulgar and pathetic. The scene may have been more tolerable in the Victorian age, when clothes were severer, or more elaborate than they are now; but even then one must have felt the human inadequacy in these surroundings – a matter Mark Twain and the English humorists felt hilariously about the whole Gothic infatuation. But when, suddenly, a loud voice calls out, 'The Speaker', and another voice calls out sharply, 'Hats off', there is a silence in which one realises that what is about to happen is not a joke at all. One is going to see the ghosts walk. One hears their rapid step. They go by in their black with the briskness of a dream and give a cold thrill for a second or two to the blood. Exactly at half past two, in perfect step, expressionless, chins a little raised, as if on some duty, exalted and exquisitely unnecessary, five men go by, dressed in black: the Sergeant-at-Arms; the mace-bearer, holding the mace before him; the wigged Speaker himself, in black silk knee-breeches and buckled shoes; his train-bearer, holding up his short robe; and his chaplain, bringing up the rear. A stir of air follows them. They have vanished. The strange moment, with no clowning in it, is eerie; it is one of London's brilliant little set pieces. In twenty seconds the 'thing' has been 'done'.

And of these sideshows and pageants, it must be said that no one ever looks an idiot in them; in a flash any Londoner appears to have the self-suppressing art of becoming his office or role; not having to act it because it is, in fact, a dormant part of his nature. The performance does not lumber along; it is as swift as wit. If in nothing else, as institutional man the Londoner is a very considerable artist. London does many things badly, but State occasions never. (Or, more strictly speaking, only once a year: the shameful hobbledehoy nonsense of the Lord Mayor's show, with its awful democratic-commercial overtones and clumsy humours.) Again, foreigners obligingly tell us that the levels of articulacy and debate in the House of Commons are higher than in other popular assemblies: if that is so, the world level must be low, for we can all remember prosaic sessions in the House, bear-garden scenes and hours of platitude. The House is simply one more club to slump into; occasionally it wakes up; always it produces its well-known characters, its notorious and tenacious bores, its simple clowns. When the Speaker in his silken breeches announces a speech by one of these, both sides of the House will unite in a roar of delighted ironical cheering. The idiots, the well-known pains in the neck get a lyrical welcome which is deeply Cockney; in the same mood were those happy cheers of the anti-aircraft gunners during the war whenever a German raider shot down one of London's barrage balloons. As a cross section of the English people, from the asinine to the intelligent, the House is appallingly representative. But two things give the debaters a valuable discipline: the historic formalities of address, which are, in themselves, exercises in elocution, and the inexhaustible devices of traditional procedure, which are the high tests of political ingenuity. The Member finds he is in a play. He must not only express his opinion, he must play his part. And at Question Time, he is up against top performers in riposte, who can make a short Johnsonian 'No, sir' mortal.

The wit, of course, is club wit; the soaring flights, the rages, the rapid-fire epigrams and knock-about comedy of the Irish Dail are not for London, nor is the rhetoric of Paris. We are not geniuses; we are simply – members. And to hear the old cries of ''vide, 'vide', or, when the House rises, the shout, centuries old, of 'Who goes home?' is comforting: London deifies its habits.

Parliament for our institutional talents; across the street, in the blackened Abbey, the whispering of the dead. The nation enshrines itself and dwarfs its own religion in the Abbey. It is the most French of our cathedrals, a monument to the Norman strain, built high in the nave in the fashion of the French cathedral builders. London has given to it the things of this world; for whereas in the cathedrals of the Continent, the Church intervenes between God and man, at Westminster the intervener, indeed the firmly presuming partner, is the Nation. The Abbey is the burial place of kings and queens (though not all the monarchs of England are buried here) and of many great men and women. It has been called the national Valhalla, the shrine and, by those who think the hundreds of monuments have ruined it, a waxworks – a sort of Notre Dame into which Madame Tussaud's and Père Lachaise have been moved. One has only to see a coronation, a Royal wedding or funeral issuing from the Abbey to see that the pageantry and symbolism, which elsewhere are in the gift of religion, are here the princely offspring of the marriage of Church and State. When Henry VIII stole the faith and vested it in the Crown, the transference was permanent, and Westminster embodies it. There *is* a light, soaring, stupendous spirit in the Abbey, but it is royal rather than divine; for this reason, one is more conscious of the inescapable frosts of time, change and mortality than of the hunger for paradise and eternal life. I doubt if there is any great cathedral in the world where one feels less the awe of God and more the awe of mundane fate; where one feels closer to the attainted business of life and persons, in age after age, than to the communion of saints. In no other cathedral is one so conscious of the dead and of the families of the dead; one might be standing at a rehearsal for the resurrection.

Mass society destroys the things it is told are its inheritance. It is rarely possible to see the Abbey without being sur-rounded by thousands of tourists from all over the world. Like St Peter's at Rome, it has been turned into a sinister sort of railway terminal. The aisles are as crowded as the pavements of Oxford Street or the alleys of a large shop, imagination is jostled, awe dispersed, and the mind never at rest. All great things, in our time, can only be seen in fragments, by fragmentary people. The place is a market, museum and palace, and of that one cannot complain, for the vast population of statuary, busts, urns and memorials rises all round the walls and seems to be climbing to the roof. The dead crowd. They stand their ground, united as if in a claim to property; in the manner of that lady in a church outside the city of Chester of whom the memorial says, 'Having made a correct estimate of the heavenly riches she decided to enter into her inheritance.' Yet if the awe is worldly, the memorials vigorously assert the pride of family, career, fame, courage and virtue – in short, the pride in life and character. It is true that a great number of the people commemorated up to the seventies of the last century are nonentities, there merely by right of birth or the paying of a large fee to the chapter. The eyes of Blake blaze out of a pillar by Poets' Corner and one can hear his words, uttered in every generation of Englishmen, from the days of Piers Plowman:

> The Enquiry in England is not whether a man has
> >Talent and Genius,
> But whether he is Passive and Polite and a Virtuous ass
> As obedient to Noblemen's opinions in Art and Science.
> If he is, he is a Good man. If not, he must be starved.

In this light, many of the memorials are a scandal; one is staggered by the very English display of shameless regard for social station. We are more than class snobs; we are death snobs. Yet there are fine things, curious things and famous figures and some pieces of excellent sculpture in the Abbey. The diversity itself is annealing. The Argyll monument, the extraordinary tomb of the Duke of Newcastle impress; the large figure of Newton seated by the globe, which is delicately engraved with the course of the comet of 1680 passing through the sportive signs of the zodiac, is a masterpiece. Chatham displays the ruling mind; Congreve has his debonair bust in a corner above Lady Holland's touching inscription. The Victorian politicians, in soapy ivory, stand outsize in gesticulation to an audience that is in the grave and, in the end, freeze our smiles and stop our whispers. They jostle and keep up the muddle and rough and tumble of life; there is a humility in the State's confusion, in its inability to impose order or a single style on a pushing Nation. And, once more, as at St Paul's, one sees the price of empire, exploration, seamanship, colonial war and adventure in those tablets to young commanders, struck by fevers and wounds far overseas, in the monuments commemorating the Briton as a proconsul. In its very chaos, in the clamour of the heroes and the office holders, Westminster records the Londoner as a man given to authority and dramatic action. It is native to London that this gathering of history should look as accidental as a junk shop. If London manners have been thought kind but abrupt, this offhandedness in the disposition of the famous or the privileged is natural to the city and indeed to the nation. But there are none who stand in the Henry VII Chapel and look up at the arms of the Knights of the Bath, and at the gloriously embroidered roof, who do not gasp with admiration. Historians and novelists have made us, and indeed a great deal of the world beyond us, familiar with stories of the kings and queens buried here; one goes in with a mind addled by literature; but the sight of the stones, the tombs, the figures themselves brings one the cold shock straight from the past. Here is beauty as others have conceived it, grace that we had forgotten, riches we had not estimated, genius and fashion of a time long gone, before our eyes. What the Londoner closed his eyes to for many generations, and especially at the climax of power, is that the most beautiful things in Westminster belong to the time when the country had its closest connection with Europe.

6

ONE SPRIGHTLY MORNING in the early summer of 1916 ten or twenty small German bombers appeared over London, looking like gnats. We rushed up to the roof of the warehouse where I worked to watch this novelty, with excitement. They dropped a few bombs, killed some horses in Billingsgate and turned Cloth Fair, Cheapside and Aldersgate into rivers of broken glass. Afterwards, outside a public house at the bottom of St Mary at Hill, a bedraggled woman singer celebrated the raid by singing an Edwardian ballad, 'City of Laughter, City of Tears', in that howling, hiccupping manner which London singing usually has.

On this morning Great Britain ceased to be an island. London, for centuries invulnerable behind its nasty seas and its fogs, was at last exposed to attack from Europe. By the time the war was over in 1918, the City had lost its overseas investments to the United States and was no longer the world's chief capital market. London's knowledge and cleverness would count, but its predominance had gone. Before 1940 its Empire had become a Commonwealth, and by 1946 most of the remains of Empire were peacefully handed over to the inhabitants. Since then London has been no more than the capital of a minor power, still rich because it has got brains and a long stocking, but with a voice that is swamped where it once ruled, flattered with hollow sentiments by condescending friends, abused for having once been great, derided because it does not behave in the ruthless manner of a Palmerston or a Disraeli. It is odd to hear our old imperialist habits praised and regarded with nostalgia by foreigners who once abused us for them. The mood of ruling London is nowadays black. In a morose way it despairs of the world, agrees to 'do its best' without much confidence in events and almost none in the way they are handled. We are apt to fall back on our moral entrench-ments, and, as Taine observed, we are a self-centred people. Our Empire was a trader's Empire, maintained by very few troops; and traders have a persistent belief that man lives not by bread alone, but by negotiation. 'You are a stupid nation,' a judge from Beirut said to me, last month. 'Your successes were never due to your brains. You achieved them because you have "character".'

I am old enough to have known three distinctive periods of London life. I have ridden in a horse tram. I have been run over by a hansom cab. I have heard the muffin bell and watched those scores of hopeful London lads, dressed in white jackets by the City of London, running into the traffic to brush up the horse manure. I have lived through the raffish, revolutionary, angry London of the twenties and thirties, watched that identifiable thread of single workless figures mooching, twenty yards apart and not speaking to one another, from shop window to shop window: the unemployed. Street singers still made the London Sunday afternoon a misery at that time. And in the spiritless streets of Bloomsbury the 'window bang' seller used to traipse by on windy days, offering us those sausages of cloth to put on our window sashes to keep out the ruling fiend of London life: the draught. (Meteorologists point out that it is truer to call the London climate windy rather than rainy.) And then – if it is possible for anyone over the age of thirty-five to know it – I have known the gaudy birth of contemporary London, the affluent.

After 1919, the Victorian mansions closed in Mayfair and Belgravia. They were turned into flats and offices. The suburban mansions of Hampstead, Richmond, Chislehurst, Beckenham and Blackheath soon went the same way. After 1945, smart society moved into small houses in Chelsea. Private wealth is still remarkable, and indignantly opposed to planning the city, for a lot of its money comes from untaxed capital gains. Property still goes in for the old London practice of 'improving' what exists. But a vast amount of the place has been torn down by bombs or man, and if the new London is notable for anything, it is for the new domestic architecture. It is rarely rankly bad; it is often good. It is also various and pleasing to the eye. Not for many generations has London paid so much attention to the living conditions of its own people. In fifty years I have seen the poor become far better off. Outside the middle class, the inhabitants of London fed far worse in 1900 than they had in the eighteenth century and the days of Gin Alley. From 1945 onwards – and, in fact, since 1940 – they eat exceedingly well. A very large number are far better housed and are far healthier. The new schools are very fine. Foreigners who have known London for thirty years tell me that the most remarkable change is in the children: they are all now well-dressed and -shod, healthy and well-fed. Compared with the children of the twenties and thirties they are a new race. Victorian charity has been replaced by the welfare services and we are redeeming the terrible sins of the nineteenth century and fulfilling the hopes of our traditions of rebellion and dissent. No longer great and imposing on the world, we have turned to ourselves.

In saying things like this we agree that London is doing no more than is being done in most other countries in Western and Eastern Europe, indeed in the world generally. London has never been as different from the cities of Western Europe as imperialists liked to think. It shared, for example, in that great burst of creative power that distinguished Europe up to 1914; it shared also in the alternations of revolt and apathy that followed. This apathy was at its worst in the twenties and thirties. London's real revolution took place during World War II. But there was one revivifying influence that cannot be ignored: the arrival of the refugees in the thirties. London has been the traditional refuge of European exiles from the time of Spanish totalitarianism in the seventeenth century, when the refugees from Holland came in and brought their talents to the weaving industry. Negro slavery was made illegal at the word of a mere magistrate on the London bench in the eighteenth century. The French émigrés, the intellectuals from Russia, Germany, France and all Europe came here after 1848. It was in London that Karl Marx worked, and it is partly from his analysis of industrial capitalism in Great Britain that *Das Kapital* sprang. Our immigrants were not, in these times, the masses; they were the talented. Our only mass immigrations were from Ireland and the Jewish peoples of Eastern Europe. In the thirties, after a long interval, the talented started to come once again. They brought new life to a place that had become colourless, as the Victorian drama declined. London at last made contact again with the fertilising sources of the Continent. The Germans, the Jews, the Austrians, the Czechs, the Italians and the Spaniards came in their thousands to us. They settled in the shabby districts where their forebears had lived three generations or more before. (One thinks of Herzen and his circle on Primrose Hill, the Italian intellectuals in the cafés and shops of Soho, the Central Europeans in the cheaper villas of Hampstead.) These neighbourhoods at once brightened. Restaurants and clubs, continental shops, appeared. The refugees kept later hours than London did, lived more outside the home, gave an alternative to our set domestic habits, provoked us politically, intellectually and in the arts. The refugees found Londoners kind, gentle and standoffish; the foreigner was left somewhat alone. He was lonely, but he was astonished that he was not interfered with. There was an old joke about having to show your passport when you got out of the tube at Belsize Park tube station. If London is a hundred times gayer today, more tolerant and civilised, than it was in the thirties, the revival owes a lot to that invasion.

The war intensified foreign influence. London was packed with foreign troops and civilians and claimed to be the centre of what was left of Europe's intellectual life – that is not saying much – and after the war, mass immigrations began. The Cypriots poured in, and they enliven every London district now; the Hungarians came; the Italians work on the London building sites; and I say nothing of the tens of thousands of foreign students from all over the world. Before the war our large student population was predominantly Indian, Pakistani and Chinese; they were all over Bloomsbury and South Kensington. They are probably now outnumbered by other races.

Finally we have had the mass immigration of West Indians, and for the first time, outside the dock areas, London has a large and ubiquitous coloured population. They are bus conductors, porters, work on the railways, in factories, in shops and warehouses. In Brixton they have their own tropical market. Around Notting Hill Gate, in Deptford, in parts of Camden Town, whole quarters belong to them. There are underlying racial jealousies and there have been ugly outbursts, mainly arising from the housing shortage. But London assimilates; there is a certain amount of intermarriage in all classes. A marked number of West Indians are students. There is also a large number of African students from the new independent states.

In short, London is now far more cosmopolitan and foreign in character than it has ever been. To a Mr Podsnap it would seem hardly British at all. He would at once join those who say it has been Americanised – in this resembling every other city in the world. He would point to the ubiquitous American phraseology: a London chophouse now becomes a Steak House, a sandwich bar becomes a Snack Bar; a restaurant becomes a Chicken Inn (has it been observed that in the sixteenth century a diet of chicken was regarded as starvation food for the poor?), and the general spread of American idiom in all classes and of American dress among teenagers. I am enough of a Podsnap myself to think our own native names, words and habits were good enough and contain an individuality that one does not want to see smoothed away. But in fact, Americanisation is superficial; at its most intense it is confined to the tourist areas; at its most beglamourising it is a fashion of adolescence. The Americanised child or youth slowly grows back into the conservative London pattern. He has to; London is his world.

One of the paradoxes of London's loss of colonial power is that it has made the contact with the people of the former colonies more intimate. In the past our never very large army of civil servants went out to these countries and the best of these men did, in fact, have a close knowledge of the place they were ruling. But now the traffic has been reversed. The people of these countries now come to London on terms of political, intellectual and social equality. The Londoner has become the servant where he was once the master and he has the experienced servant's influence. In the past, the former colonial saw the Englishman as a privileged and aloof stranger who was cut off from him; in London, he finds the mass of ordinary Londoners are people not so vastly different from himself. The empire builder at home is a very different person from the empire builder abroad; and, at home, without an empire, he still has his traditional concern, which goes back centuries, for the world beyond his shores. It is the ineradicable part of the island mind. We had (the Beirut judge said) 'character'. Is that being worn away as London becomes indistinguishable from the other conurbations of the world? Does the technological revolution inevitably depersonalise and create vast anonymous populations? And if London does retain its individual quality, will that be just a picturesque nuisance, a superfluous eccentricity? Who knows! The outside world has not, even yet, caught up with the fact that the Londoner was not a cold, strong, impassive upper-class dandy. The mass of Londoners are now very much in power and they display the perennial traits of self-dramatisation, heartiness, level-headedness and swank.

Modern cities are built for the night; then prison architecture becomes tolerable. In my childhood and youth the centre of London was most memorable for its shadows. The whitish or greenish gaslight was soft, gently illuminating a window or two, casting a tent of misty shadow round the pool of light beneath. The people in the streets appeared out of one shadow and presently vanished into the next. The city was mysterious, and soft to the eye. Occasionally in the East End, in the alleys of the docks, or around St James's, where a lamplighter still goes round on his bicycle every night, one walks into the shadows of this old London. But the rest is rank with electricity, and the shadows have gone. Flying into London at night one looks down on a jewelled place, criss-crossed by chains of sodium or toffee-coloured lights and bloodied by neon. Waiting for your bus under the lamp standard your skin takes on a corpse-like quality – perhaps, in our kind of world, prophetic.

This cruel and clinical light exposes. The London crowd looks almost dangerous and garish in the pleasure quarters; and, indeed, crime no longer springs from the shadows but is lit up. The hoodlums who attack the West Indians in Notting Hill Gate with broken milk bottles – an old London weapon – the man who coshes the elderly club member on his own doorstep in a crowded street at eleven at night, do so in the floodlit street. At first the thousands at night look foreign; the sallow and swarthy seem to outnumber the red-faced English, until one discovers that many of the swarthy are English too; one can no longer speak certainly of London types. What has really happened is that a new breed of Londoners has appeared. They are very young and, for the first time for many generations, they cultivate a romantic style. It is partly Italianate, partly American. It is now more elegant than 'beat'; around Notting Hill Gate, the hoodlums wear black leather jackets, narrow trousers, deeply turned up over soft black shoes with high uppers; they sport side-burns and wear rings, charms and medallions. But the Edwardian revival affects all classes of the young – not to mention the Prime Minister. I have seen a few walking sticks lately. Are they on the way 'in' again, after fifty years? The new dandyism is different from earlier manifestations; it comes, significantly, from below, not from above, and, like all fashions, is a protest. The speech of the mass of younger Londoners is a mixture of BBC English, Americanisms, and is rarely Cockney of the old rapid, jaunty manner, although Cockney rhyming slang is, I would guess, on the increase among porters, lorry drivers and warehousemen. 'Titfer' for hat, 'barnet' for hair, 'plates' for feet are very common. ('Spades' – the word for coloured men – is not rhyming slang.) Ordinary speech of the kind you hear on top of a bus is becoming a peculiar slither of adenoidal vowels and no consonants, and is incomprehensible to those not well up on pop singing, jazz, the catchwords of psychology and the lore of television. A good deal of London talk is buried quotation, and it is hard to know whether the cheerful interchange I heard between a doorman and a fat hearty old soul at the British Museum yesterday is invention or something the parties had heard on television:

DOORMAN: Meet you tonight, ducks?
HEARTY SOUL: Who? Me? Under the gooseberry bush? You'd be afraid.

This popular rough stuff appeared, of course, in the sixteenth-century plays, for the Cockney's tongue has always wagged coarsely and lewdly. But as you listen to the deformations of modern speech, you can tell that you are hearing the first generation of an oral culture, a language picked up by ear and with only a fading, half-hearted connection with the printed page.

London no longer belongs to the 'nobs' and the 'toffs'; it belongs to the crowd. If the 'nobs' no longer go to their clubs, but turn up in the Chelsea pubs, they are careful to put on their pullovers, their cavalry twill, their unsporting sporting clothes. The crowd has set the tone. The once silent squares in the centre fill up every night with motor coaches that bring trippers from the provinces by tens of thousands. They come to bathe in neon, and London drains the life from all England. A city like Manchester is dead after seven. The crowd rolls into the pubs and the coffee bars where it is waited on by Cypriots, Italians and Germans. It pushes into the striptease clubs and the clip joints where the girls claim to be hospital nurses by day and, in fact, often are. The notorious swarm of prostitutes has been driven off the streets and relies on small ads in shop windows offering massage, dancing lessons, modelling; they signal from windows. Lately they are venturing once more into doorways. Popular taste runs less to the old London gaudiness and loudness than to Edwardian or Regency chichi. Many of the new 'democratic' pubs where the separate bars have been abolished are dolled up with arty iron and glass work, coloured glasses, artificial flowers, fake Toby jugs, plushy wallpapers and chains of coloured lights. Thank heaven there are plenty of simple places, in the old varnish and mahogany, some with the beautifully etched Victorian glass and lettering, where one meets the old mild pomposities, where one can be reassured by an aspidistra and a stout barmaid who calls you 'love' or 'dear' and overfeeds her dog.

And in the common London of the buses, cheap shops, bars, you are always 'dear' or 'love'. It is all 'What's yours, love?' 'Where to, dear?' 'Here you are, ducks' to man, woman or child. One lives in an ooze of affection. But hard, sharp-eyed, kind, sentimental London always keeps its head and, in a crisis, resorts at once to the stern mask of respectability. I know nothing more indicative of the London temper than the change in the faces, the shocked silence, the look of moral *de haut en bas* that comes over any collection of us when, publicly, 'something' happens. 'Something' absolutely must *not* happen in this room, office, cinema, bar, street. We are appalled – unless, of course, the 'something' has happened to a dog, and then all our passion is roused and, in chorus, we go mad and address the whole world with indignation. Until someone utters that healing moral phrase that must be spoken a million times a day on the London streets and that will instantly cure our panic: 'It's wrong. It's not right. It's all wrong.' Except in the matter of what happens to dogs, cats, horses, budgerigars and canaries, London is the least nervous city in the world.

DAUNT BOOKS

Founded in 2010, the Daunt Books imprint is dedicated
to discovering brilliant works by talented authors from
around the world. Whether reissuing beautiful new
editions of lost classics or introducing fresh literary
voices, we're drawn to writing that evokes a strong
sense of place – novels, short fiction, memoirs, travel
accounts, and translations with a lingering atmosphere,
a thrilling story, and a distinctive style. With our
roots as a travel bookshop, the titles we publish
are inspired by the Daunt shops themselves,
and the exciting atmosphere of discovery
to be found in a good bookshop.

For more information, please visit
www.dauntbookspublishing.co.uk

V. S. PRITCHETT (1900–1997) lived in London for more than eighty years. He was literary editor of the *New Statesman* and the *Nation*, frequently contributed to the *New York Times Book Review*, and his fiction often appeared in *The New Yorker*. He received numerous awards including the 1969 Heinemann Award, the 1974 PEN Award, and the 1993 Golden Pen Award.